NEW ENGLAND'S GREATEST BOXERS

NEW ENGLAND'S GREATEST BOXERS

Bob Trieger

Copyright © 2022 by Bob Trieger.

Library of Congress Control Number: 2022914974
ISBN: Hardcover 978-1-6698-3714-5
Softcover 978-1-6698-3713-8
eBook 978-1-6698-3712-1

All rights reserved. No part of this book may be reproduced or transmitted in any form or by any means, electronic or mechanical, including photocopying, recording, or by any information storage and retrieval system, without permission in writing from the copyright owner.

Any people depicted in stock imagery provided by Getty Images are models, and such images are being used for illustrative purposes only.
Certain stock imagery © Getty Images.

Print information available on the last page.

Rev. date: 08/09/2022

To order additional copies of this book, contact:
Xlibris
844-714-8691
www.Xlibris.com
Orders@Xlibris.com
844422

*Dedicated to my wife Terri, daughter Caitlin,
and grandchildren Amelia and Leo*

CONTENTS

Introduction ix
1. Willie Pep 1
2. Rocky Marciano 6
3. Marvin Hagler 11
4. Sandy Saddler 18
5. Sam Langford 22
6. John L. Sullivan 26
7. Vinny Pazienza 30
8. Tony Demarco 37
9. Jack Sharkey 41
10. Paul Pender 47
11. Marlon Starling 52
12. Chad Dawson 58
13. Kid Kaplan 64
14. Lou Bruillard 67
15. John Ruiz 70
16. George Dixon 77
17. Joe Walcott 80
18. Demetrius Andrade 84
19. Jack Delaney 92
20. Battling Battalino 97

21.	Cocoa Kid	101
22.	Travis Simms	105
23.	Jose Antonio Rivera	113
24.	Joey Gamache	120
25.	Micky Ward	125

Honorable Mentions.. 135
World Championship Fights By Top New England Fighters.......... 141
The Ring's Top 100... 153
New England's Greatest Boxers In The International Boxing
Hal Of Fame.. 157
Photo Gallery Layout & Credits.. 159

INTRODUCTION

New England's Greatest Boxers was a special project for me that started a long, long time ago. As a youngster, I watched *Gillette Cavalcade of Sports* every Friday night with my father. My first recollection of boxing is from 1962, the tragic Emile Griffith-Benny "The Kid" Paret fight, in which Griffith brutally pounded Paret into a coma from which he never came out, dying a few weeks later. I'm not sure what that says about me, but I had officially been bitten by the boxing bug, and still remain an invested boxing fan. In 1975, I started writing about boxing for several newspapers in the Boston area, and twenty-five years later I founded Full Court PRESS, a Boston-based combat sports publicity agency specializing in boxing.

I was fortunate to learn from some of best in the boxing business, starting with Al Lacy, a boxing trainer from Chelsea (MA) who I later worked with at Wonderland Greyhound Park, which also was a popular closed-circuit site for major boxing events in the 1990s, as well as hosting professional boxing events featuring future world champions such a John Ruiz and Shannon Briggs. Lacy trained world champions in five consecutive decades, including two members of "New England's Greatest Boxers," Jack Sharkey and Paul Pender. I became a sponge, listening to Al every night for one complete summer, taking it all in from one of the best boxing trainers of all time.

I eventually realized that, for a sport without character, boxing had a wealth of colorful characters. And despite countless predictions that boxing was eminently dead, the "Sweet Science" would survive because people would always be interested in watching, as well as betting, whenever two people fight. Its popularity is cyclable; after all, boxing is the second oldest profession.

I also discovered that different boxing eras were dominated by the lowest ethnic groups on the economic ladder of society: Irish, Italians, and Jews ruled in the late 1800s and early 1900s; blacks through much of the twentieth century; and more recently, Latinos and those from former Soviet Bloc countries.

Boxing has always been the passageway to a better life for most of its participants, who risk their lives every time they fight.

Boxing is also the loneliest and most unforgiving sport; two people wearing only gloves, trunks, and shoes, trying to concuss each other under bright lights in a four-corned square, risking death every time they go up those three stairs. Unfortunately, at least during modern times, a loss is extremely difficult to bounce back from, ultimately requiring the fighter to practically battle his or her way back up the competitive ladder once again.

I actually started nearer the top of the sport than struggling upward from the depths of club shows. My first two fighter clients, John "The Quietman" Ruiz and "Irish" Micky Ward, respectively, absolutely spoiled me from the start. I was driven around Las Vegas and Atlantic City in stretch limousines, dined at five-star restaurants, and stayed in beautiful casinos. Then I handled publicity for Kevin "The Clones Colossus" McBride, who knocked Mike Tyson out and into retirement.

I've been the personal publicist for nine world champions (WBC, WBA, WBO, and IBF only) during their respective reigns, as well as worked thirty-six world title fights; and traveled to Kazakhstan, Brazil, and Brazil for work, in addition to eighteen different US states and Washington, DC—all thanks to boxing.

Somewhere along my pugilistic ride, I realized comparing generational boxers was so subjective that it was virtually impossible to rank the top twenty-five New England boxers of all time, at least in terms of thoroughly pleasing the public. Too many factors play a major role in figuring out which boxers were better than others: different weight classes (only eight compared to seventeen today); technological advantages of training, diet, advanced equipment; more lucrative purses, media attention, and more.

Sure, maybe it's like comparing apples and oranges, but what a terrific debate, or more often than not, lively argument this controversial, subjective subject inevitably leads to for New England boxing fans. Everybody has his or her favorites, whether it's because of their specific era of interest, ethnicity, or relatability. Ask a boxing fan at any event, watching a fight on television in a barroom, or wearing a boxer's merchandise while working out in a gym. No two people feel the same about discussing who they believe is greater in terms of ranks in order, top to bottom. I tried to look at this book with a simple qualifier: who would I rather have been, provided everything was equal, like mythical pound for pound ratings, if they fought each other.

I also wanted to ensure that each was a true New England fighter, not somebody who merely lived in the six-state region for a short period of time, because we New Englanders are truly provincial. The one rule I had in terms of eligibility was they had to either have been born in New England or lived there for a minimum of five years during the height of their professional careers. Gene Tunney, "Slapsie" Maxie Rosenbloom, and Beau Jack are boxers referred to by some as New England fighters, but they were declared ineligible for this project because they were neither born nor lived in New England for a minimum of five years during their pro careers.

I remember reading the late great Bert Randolph Sugar's book *Boxing's Greatest Fighters*, greatly appreciating how difficult it must have been for him to list his top one hundred boxers of all time. In fact, admittedly, I used Sugar's book as a quasi-template for this book.

Who ranks where often leads to rather loud talks, sometimes fisticuffs, about who the best ever are from New England. Now, I'm not egotistical enough to believe I'm the preeminent expert on New England's boxing history, not by any means, but I am a historian of this subject to some degree. I wanted to write a book ranking New England's greatest boxers, but I continually procrastinated, claiming I needed sufficient time to properly devote to extensive researching and writing I simply didn't have due to my everyday workload.

Well, the COVID-19 pandemic of 2020 completely blew that excuse for me. I had plenty of time, and figured it would be a fun project. I asked a group of well-informed New England boxing individuals—promoters, matchmakers, media, fans, managers/advisers, announcers, photographers, trainers, strength coaches, and boxing attorneys—to vote for their top twenty-five New England boxers in order of their preferences, and I developed a scoring system to determine the final list. Accomplishments as well as contributions to the sport of boxing were guidelines for selection.

I want to be completely transparent, avoiding any thoughts of my possible favoritism, noting up front that I've been the personal publicist for some of the top twenty-five: John Ruiz, Demetrius Andrade, Jose Antonio Rivera, and Micky Ward. I have also met, known, and/or have worked fights featuring Marvelous Marvin Hagler, Vinny Paz, Tony DeMarco, Chad Dawson, Travis Simms, and Joey Gamache.

Boxing was held in Boston on a regular basis during the "Glory Years" at legendary venues like the Boston Garden, Boston Arena, Mechanics Hall, Fenway Park, Braves Field, and Hynes Auditorium. Massachusetts also had Memorial Hall in Lowell and the Valley Arena Garden in Holyoke for boxing. Rhode Island had the R.I. Convention Center and Providence Civic Center; Connecticut the New Haven Arena, Hartford Civic Center and Hartford Coliseum, plus the Portland Auditorium in New Hampshire and The Colisée in Maine. And Foxwoods Resort Casino and later Mohegan Sun hosted many of boxing's marquee boxing events during the late twentieth into the twenty-first century.

Over time many of boxing's all-time greats fought throughout New England. "Sugar" Ray Robinson was a frequent guest with eighteen fights in Massachusetts (twelve), Connecticut (two), Rhode Island (two), and Maine (two). In their infamous rematch in 1965, Muhammad Ali knocked out Sonny Liston in the opening round in Lewiston, Maine.

Floyd Mayweather, Roy Jones, Julio Cesar Chavez, Pernell Whitaker, and Evander Holyfield fought at Foxwoods; Sugar Ray Leonard boxed seven times in New England. Boxing was banned during the early part of the twentieth century throughout most of the United States, excluding an ordinance sanctioning the "Sweet Science" in Chelsea, Massachusetts, which hosted fights headlined by the likes of Jack Johnson and Abe Attell, among the more notables.

Other greats who fought as least once as a professional in New England include Joe Louis, Harry Greb, Benny Leonard, Micky Walker, Tony Canzoneri, Gene Tunny, Jimmy Wilde, Archie Moore, Joe Gans, Stanley Ketchell, Ezzard Charles, Jake LaMotta, Emile Griffith, Terry McGovern, Billy Conn, Kid Chocolate, Carmen Basilio, and Bob Fitzsimmons.

The battle for the no. 1 spot in the rankings was a two-fighter race from the start. Pep eventually edged Marciano, who technical accounted for one more first-place votes than Pep. Hagler had two and Sullivan one. The next four in the final top twenty-five (Hagler, Sandy Saddler, Langford, and Sullivan) were consensus selections, if not exactly, some in slightly different orders of preference.

Fifteen of the top twenty-five are inducted into the International Boxing Hall of Fame (IBHOF); all but Langford, Cocoa Kid, and Ward (he won WBU light welterweight crown) were major world title holders; four are inducted into the Italian American Sports Hall of Fame (Pep, Marciano, Vinny Paz, and Tony DeMarco); Kid Kaplan's in the International Sports Hall of Fame; and Andrade is the lone Olympian.

Southern New England dominates the top twenty-five: Massachusetts has fourteen representatives, Connecticut eight, and Rhode Island two. Maine had one (Gamache) and New Hampshire and Vermont were shut out. Team New England combined for a total of forty-three major world titles. Only the four major sanctioning bodies from in recent history—World Boxing Council (WBC), World Boxing Association (WBA), International Boxing Federation (IBF), and World Boxing Organization (WBO)—were considered for this project. Special thanks to boxrec.com, boxing's official record keeper, for its data used throughout this book, along with *The Ring* magazine and International Boxing Hall of Fame (IBHOF).

Sadly, Hagler and DeMarco passed away during the time between top twenty-five selections and publishing this book.

xliii

This project turned out to be a labor of love, in addition to supplying fun for everybody involved, especially when we were all under quarantine. I'd like to thank the following people, in no particular order, for assisting me by taking the time to research and submit their selections in order of their particular preference: Jimmy Burchfield Sr., Mike Mazulli, Bob Yalen, Ted Panagiotis, Mark Vaz, Chuck Shear, John Vena, Steve Tobey, Ron Borges, Peter Czymbor, Bobby Russo, Tony Cardinale, Ian Cannon, Ted Sares, Mike Marley, Mike Moynihan, and Keith McGrath.

Yalen and Borges were inducted into the IBHOF Class of 2021.

My friend dating back to my preteens growing up in Brighton, Mike Marley, died in 2022. He is the reason I got into writing, and I will always owe him a great debt. I lived in the Fidelis Way projects; he was from nearby Oak Square. We were classmates at Taft Junior High and Brighton High.

Mike wrote for *The Ring* magazine as a twelve-year-old, and was president of the Cassius Clay Fan Club (250,000 members) in 1966. One day, he asked if I wanted to join him that evening at Boston City Hospital when he visited the world heavyweight champion, now named Muhammad Ali, who had had an appendectomy, postponing his second fight against Sonny Liston, which later moved from Boston to Lewiston, Maine. I thought Mike was exaggerating his relationship with Ali, and politely explained that I couldn't go with him because I had a night paper route. I did but I should have taken the night off because a friend took my place and visited with Ali all night. One of my biggest regrets in life is passing on the opportunity to meet "The Greatest" up close and personal.

A bombastic public relations director for Don King, Marley was a prolific writer for the *New York Post*, *Las Vegas Sun*, *Nevada State Journal*, and other publications, and five-time Emmy Award-winning producer of Howard Cosell's ABC *SportsBeat*. Mike managed future world champions Shannon Briggs, Robert Garcia, Terry Norris, and James "Bonechrusher" Smith. He also served as an advisor, matchmaker, and promoter in boxing. In his early forties, Mike became a criminal lawyer in New York City, where he lived the majority of his adult life.

It was always great to see Mike at boxing events in New York City, Boston, and Las Vegas.

Marley wrote about me when I was playing basketball and baseball for Brighton High. When he left to attend the University of Nevada at Reno, Mike encouraged me to take over for him as the sportswriter for the *Allston-Brighton Citizen Item*. In high school, we flunked Spanish II together, and ironically, I also didn't pass English class as a senior. Odd that I'd become a writer, but Mike said I knew sports and he recommended that I just write like I talked. And that's precisely what I've done all these years, culminating with this book. I've never looked back.

The final top twenty-five truly stands for New England's all-time greatest professional boxers. Their respective rankings, of course, will also be debatable, so let the arguments and discourse begin!

Bob Trieger
Salem, Massachusetts

No. 1

WILLIE PEP

"The Will o' the Wisp"
Simply the Best

Considered as one of the best pure boxers of all-time, two-time World Featherweight Champion Willie "Will o' the Wisp" Pep (229-11-1, 65 KOs) is New England's all-time greatest boxer, based on his magnificent body of work during his twenty-six-year incredible career.

The Connecticut fighter, born in Middletown and fighting out of Rock Hill, was 11-3 (5 KOs) in world title fights, defeating six world champions, including Hall of Famers Sandy Saddler (Pep's archrival) and Manuel Ortiz, as well as Jackie Wilson (2), Sal Bartolo (3), Phil Terranova, and Paddy DeMarco. Pep holds his own against any featherweight star from his era right through contemporary times, including fellow New Englanders Saddler and George Dixon, along with Manny Pacquiao, Salvador Sanchez, Wilfredo Gomez, Henry Armstrong, Floyd Mayweather Jr., Abe Attell, Alexis Arguello, or any other fighter from this rich weight class. Again, Pep's overall body of work separates him from the others, especially considering the art of hitting without being hit—something Pep did better than anybody.

A two-time Connecticut State amateur champion, Pep came up around the same time as "Sugar" Ray Robinson—who Pep is often compared to regarding the greatest boxer of all time debates—and fought as amateurs in 1938. The 105-pound Pep reportedly fought the twenty-three to forty-two pounds heavier Robinson, depending on which report was most believable, upstairs at the Checkerboard Feed Co. store in Norwich, Connecticut. New York, where national Golden Gloves champion Robinson lived, didn't pay amateur boxers, so he used a pseudonym (Ray Roberts) to get some cash for his fight against Pep, who, unbelievably, was told before their fight that Robinson, whose birth name was Walker Smith, wasn't a good fighter. Pep admitted that Robinson "wiped him out that night," handing Pep his only amateur loss. Many years later the two champions fought an exhibition.

Pep made his professional debut on July 10, 1940, taking a four-round decision from James McGovern in Hartford. Pep's first twenty-five pro fights were split between his home state and Massachusetts, and he didn't fight outside of New England until his twenty-sixth fight, in which he knocked out Eddie Flores in Thompsonville, Michigan.

In 1942, Pep (41-0) won a ten-round unanimous decision against world title challenger Joey Archibald (60-31-5) at Bulkeley Stadium in Hartford, and again four months later in Providence's Rhode Island Auditorium. In late 1942, twenty-year-old Pep decisioned future Hall of Famer Chalky Wright (143-33-17) by way of a fifteen-round unanimous decision (10-4, 11-4, 11-4) at Madison Square Garden to capture the New York State Athletic Commission (NYSAC) World featherweight championship.

Pep's undefeated start in the pro ranks reached 62-0, second best ever only to Julio Cesar Chavez's 87, before another future Hall of Famer, 69-27-5 Sammy Angott, won a close ten-round unanimous decision (5-4 x 2, 6-4) in a 1943 non-title fight at Madison Square Garden, where Pep had become a semi-regular attraction. During the rest of that same year, Pep won all five of his fights, including a ten-round split decision at Boston Garden versus 45-14-6 Sal Bartolo, another world champion, once again by fifteen-round unanimous decision in Pep's first world title defense at Braves Field in Boston. Prior to this fight, Pep took a twelve-round unanimous decision from 90-24-8 Jackie Wilson in Pittsburgh.

The following year, Pep went 16-0, highlighted by a ten-round unanimous decision over 59-11-2 Manuel Ortiz and the two other decisions against Wright, the latter in a world title defense. Pep rolled through an unbeaten 1945 (8-0-1, majority draw with 39-16 Jimmy McAllister in Baltimore)—highlighted by his fifteen-round unanimous decision against 38-11-9 Phil Terranova at Madison Square Garden in a world title defense—and 1946 (17-0), punctuated by a ten-round decision against Wilson in a rematch, the world title defense knockout of Bartolo in the twelfth round at Madison Square Garden to become undisputed world featherweight champion, and a third-round knockout of Wright in Milwaukee.

Pep, in effect, actually had two pro careers. In January 1947, Pep was seriously injured in a plane crash that killed the copilot and two other passengers. Pep, with his surreal 109-1-1 record, returned to the ring on June 17, 1947, when he dropped Victor Flores twice en route to a ten-round victory on points in Hartford. A little more than two months and six fights later, Pep destroyed 58-9-4 Jock Leslie, knocking him out cold in the twelfth round in yet another world title defense. The second half of his career he was 120-10.

Legendary heavyweight champion Jack Dempsey refereed the February 24, 1948, world title fight at the Orange Bowl in Miami between defending champion Pep and challenger Humberto Sierra (40-7-3), who Pep had decisioned six months earlier in a non-title fight held in the rain. Pep decked Sierra in the second round, and Dempsey halted the fight in the tenth after Pep had floored Sierra again. Paddy DeMarco (32-2) was decisioned by Pep seven months later at Madison Square Garden.

Pep (134-1-1) lost his lineal world title on October 29, 1948, at Madison Square Garden to 86-6-2 Saddler, a fellow New Englander, and the two developed a fierce rivalry that, surprisingly, Saddler dominated with three victories in four fights. Pep was down in the third and finally in the fourth for the full count. Less than four months later, Pep regained his world title from Saddler with a fifteen-round unanimous decision (10-5, 9-6, 9-5) at Madison Square Garden in the 1947 Fight of the Year, marking the highlight of his career.

Pep successfully defended his crown with a seventh-round technical knockout of Eddie Compo (57-1-3) in Waterbury, Connecticut. Compo was knocked down twice in the fifth and again in the seventh.

Saddler regained the world title from Pep, who was unable to continue in the eighth round at Yankee Stadium after he had suffered a separated shoulder at the end of the seventh round. History repeated itself on September 26, 1951, at the Polo Grounds in one of the dirtiest fights in boxing history. Pep was unable to answer the bell to start the ninth round due to a bloody right eye that bothered him, despite him being ahead of the scorecards.

Although he fought for fifteen more years—he retired in 1959 but returned in 1965 for ten more fights—Pep never received another world title shot, and retired for good in 1966 at the age of forty-three.

A consummate boxer and defensive wizard, Pep was like a male ballet dancer in the ring, wearing gloves, trunks, and boxing shoes instead of tights and dance slippers, who in 1946 won a round against Jackie Graves without throwing a single punch. He bobbed, weaved, and feinted his way for three minutes without being struck or throwing a punch.

Willie Pep is the greatest New England boxer, and one of the best pure boxers to ever grace a ring.

ALL-NEW ENGLAND

Birth Name: Guglielmo Papaleo
Nickname: Will o' the Wisp
Born: September 19, 1922, in Middletown, Connecticut
Hometown: Rock Hill, Connecticut
Death: November 23, 2006
Amateurs: 1938–39 Connecticut State Champion
Pro Record: 229-11-1 (65 KOs, 6 KOBY)
Pro Titles: Two-time world featherweight champion (November 20, 1942–October 29, 1948; February 11, 1949–September 8, 1950)
Pro Career: 1940–66
Height: 5' 5"
Reach: 68"
Stance: Orthodox
Division: Featherweight

World Title Fight Record: 11-3 (5 KOs)

Records vs. World Champions: 13-5 (2 KOs), defeated Jackie Wilson (2), Sal Bartolo (3), Manuel Ortiz,* Phil Terranova, Paddy DeMarco, Sandy Saddler*; lost to Sammy Angott,* Sandy Saddler (3),* Kid Bassey (* International Boxing HOF)

Manager: Lou Viscusi
Trainer: Bill Gore

Notes: International Boxing Hall of Fame, Class of 1990; 1997 inducted into Italian American National Sports HOF; won 135 of first 138 fights; after he retired as a boxer, he remained in boxing as an inspector and referee; 1945 *The Ring* Fighter of the Year; broke his back in 1947 plane crash in which three died; named greatest featherweight and fifth greatest boxer of the twentieth century by Associated Press (AP); married six times; became a referee and deputy boxing commissioner in Connecticut after he retired; the movie about his life, *Pep*, started filming in late 2021

No. 2

ROCKY MARCIANO

"The Brockton Blockbuster"
Only Undefeated World Heavyweight Champ

From 1952 to 1955, Rocky Marciano ruled boxing as the world heavyweight champion, the victor in three Fights of the Year, as well as three-time Fighter of the Year (1952, 1953, and 1954), in which he defeated, in order, Harry Mathews (81-3-5) in a world heavyweight title eliminator, Jersey Joe Walcott (49-19-1) twice, Roland LaStarza (53-3), and Ezzard Charles (86-10-1) twice—the latter five matches in world title fights. Marciano was 6-0 (5 KOs) in five world title fights, and the Title Eliminator during this three-year stretch.

Marciano, who is the only world heavyweight champion to permanently retire undefeated (49-0, 43 KOs) at the relatively young age of only thirty-two, had only one knock against him in that some of the greats he fought were when they were past their respective primes, especially considering all the wear and tear they each endured: Archie Moore and Walcott at thirty-nine and Joe Louis at thirty-six.

A high school dropout who excelled in baseball and football at Brockton (MA) High School, Marciano didn't learn how to box until 1943, after he was drafted into the US Army, primarily to get out of undesirable details. But Rocky showed his natural ability to hurt and cause pain after he was discharged from the service and fought as an amateur, despite constantly being told that he was too small (5' 10.5", 185 lbs.) to become a heavyweight champion. Respect didn't come until his 1950 fight in Madison Square Garden with fellow undefeated heavyweight, 37-0 Roland LaStarza, who would come the closest in the professional ranks to defeating Marciano, who won a ten-round split decision, because of New York State's supplemental point system. The three judges, including referee Jack Watson, turned in their scorecards (5-5, 4-5, 5-4) and Watson's 9-6 supplemental score gave Marciano the victory.

In 1951, Marciano was a 6.5 to 5 underdog betting choice at Madison Square Garden, although he was nine years younger than thirty-seven-year-old Joe Louis (67-2), who hadn't been world champion in three years. Marciano floored Louis twice in the eighth round, the first from a left hook that resulted in an eight-count, and the latter sent Louis through the ropes when referee Ruby Goldstein stopped the fight without counting, unceremoniously marking the end of Louis' remarkable career. Louis was Marciano's idol, and Rocky reportedly wept in Louis' dressing room after their fight.

Marciano had climbed the ratings ladder to earn a World Heavyweight Elimination match against 81-3-5 Harry Mathews in Yankee Stadium. A pair of punishing left hooks in the second round pulled down the final curtain, and Marciano was the mandatory challenger for the world heavyweight title. His opportunity came on September 23, 1952, at Municipal Stadium in Philadelphia against defending National Boxing Association (NBA) World heavyweight champion Walcott.

Behind on the judges' scorecards (4-7, 4-8, 5-7) entering the critical thirteenth round, Marciano's nose was cut so severely, it looked like it was going to fall off. But Walcott used his trademark feint to set up his patented right hand, fondly known as "Suzie Q." Rocky beat Walcott to the punch, unloading his famous punch to land what was later known as the shot heard around the world, leaving Walcott slumped on his knees, his arm and knees dragged over the ropes, motionless long after referee Charley Daggert had counted him out.

Newly crowned world heavyweight champion, Marciano made his first title defense the following May at Chicago Stadium, knocking out Walcott in the first round of what was his final fight. Next in line was LaStarza (53-3) at Polo Grounds in New York in September 1953. Marciano had clearly learned an invaluable lesson in their first fight, and he methodically built a lead (7-3, 6-4, 5-5) in their rematch, blasting LaStarza through the ropes to stop the fight in the eleventh round in the 1953 Fight of the Year.

Marciano fought Charles (85-10-1) twice in 1954, both at the famed Yankee Stadium, winning the first title fight by way of a fifteen-round unanimous decision (8-5, 9-5, 8-6), followed by an eighth-round knockout in the 1954 Fight of the Year. Now one of the most popular athletes in the world at that time, Marciano next fought British and European champion Don Cockell (66-11-1), who was knocked out in the eighth round at San Francisco's Kezar Stadium.

The final fight of Marciano's career was delayed a day because of hurricane warnings, held September 21, 1956, against legendary Moore (149-19-8) at Yankee Stadium. Moore dropped Marciano in the second round for a four count, but Rocky recovered to record a ninth-round knockout.

On April 27, 1956, the thirty-two-year-old Marciano announced his retirement. He considered making a comeback in 1959 to challenge Ingemar Johansson, but after only a month of training, for the first time in four years, Marciano pulled the plug on his comeback. Some believed that Rocky had retired because of an arthritic right elbow and a ruptured disc in his back, while others speculated that he hung up his gloves because of his deteriorating relationship with his manager, Al Weill.

Marciano was determined to inflict damage on his opponents, willing to take three punches to land one of his own, usually a brutal shot more like a bomb exploding, thrown from his awkward style as he applied constant pressure. Marciano was a notorious puncher, so brutal in fact that Muhammad Ali complained that Marciano left him with bruised, painful arms from blocking Marciano's punches during the filming of the computer simulated film *The Superfight:*

Marciano vs. Ali, which aired in 1970. Marciano at that time, shortly before he died in a plane crash, was forty-five and he hadn't fought in fourteen years.

Rocky Marciano retired to this day as the lone world heavyweight champion with an undefeated record (49-0, 43 KOs), along with the highest knockout percentage of any world heavyweight champion: 87.76 percent during his career.

ALL-NEW ENGLAND

Birth Name:	Rocco Francis Marchegiano
Nickname:	The Brockton Blockbuster
Born:	September 1, 1923, in Brockton, Massachusetts
Hometown:	Brockton, Massachusetts
Death:	August 31, 1969
Amateurs:	9-4 (7 KOs), 1947 and 1948 Massachusetts/Rhode Island Golden Gloves, 1948 New England Tournament of Champions, and 1948 New England AAU champion, won 1946 Amateur Armed Forces Boxing Tournament while awaiting discharge from US Army
Pro Record:	49-0 (43 KOs)
Pro Titles:	World Heavyweight Champion (September 23, 1952–April 27, 1955)
Pro Career:	1947–55
Height:	5' 10.5"
Reach:	68"
Stance:	Orthodox
Division:	Heavyweight

World Title Fight Record: 7-0 (6 KOs)
Records vs. World Champions: 16-0 (6 KOs), defeated Joe Louis,* Archie Moore, Jersey Joe Walcott (2), Ezzard Charles (2) (* International Boxing HOF)

Manager:	Al Weill
Trainer:	Charley Goldman, Al Colombo

Notes: International Boxing Hall of Fame, Class of 1990; his 68" reach was shortest ever of any world heavyweight champion; son of Italian immigrants; only heavyweight to retire undefeated; caught pneumonia as a baby and nearly died; good high school football and baseball player in high school; had a tryout with Fayetteville Cubs, minor league affiliate of Chicago Cards; the day before his forty-sixth birthday, he died in a plane crash heading to Des Moines, Iowa, from Chicago for a special engagement; rumors are that Marciano didn't trust banks and that he left millions of dollars secretly buried when he died that were never found; *The Ring*'s three-time Fighter of the Year: 1952 vs. Jersey Joe Walcott II, 1953 vs. Roland LaStarza II, 1954 vs. Ezzard Charles II; named third greatest heavyweight of the twentieth century by Associated Press (AP)

No. 3

MARVIN HAGLER

"Marvelous"
Destruction & Destroy

Three-time world middleweight champion Marvelous Marvin Hagler prepared for each fight as if he were going into battle. He wore a black hat with *WAR* embroidered in white, and trained in prison-like conditions during winter months at the desolate Provincetown Inn, located at the top of Cape Cod in Provincetown, Massachusetts.

It obviously worked, as Hagler went from struggling prospect to People's Champ and ultimately inducted into the International Boxing Hall of Fame.

Born in Newark, New Jersey, the rugged southpaw moved to Brockton (MA) with his mother and siblings after their house was burned down during the infamous 1967 Newark riots. He learned how to box in 1969—after getting tuned up on the Brockton streets by a local boxer Marvin later defeated in the ring—when he walked into a local gym owned and operated by the Petronelli brothers, Goody and Pat, who became Marvin's trainers and managers throughout his glorious career.

Hagler developed into a standout amateur boxer (52-2, 43 KOs), who captured top honors at the 1973 National AAU Championship, where he was named the Most Outstanding Boxer of the tournament.

Hagler lied about his age to box, claiming he was eighteen and of legal age to fight instead of his real age (sixteen), which never became known until he legally changed his name to Marvelous Marvin Hagler in 1982. In 1973, Hagler made his pro debut, stopping Terry Ryan in the second round of their fight at Brockton High School. He was 14-0 in 1974 when he entered the WNAC-TV studio in Boston to fight Olympic gold medalist "Sugar" Ray Seales (21-0). Hagler won a ten-round unanimous decision (98-94, 97-95, 97-93), and three months later they had a rematch in Seales' hometown of Tacoma, Washington, in which the two fought to a ten-round majority draw (99-99 X 2, 96-98).

Unbeaten (25-0-1, 19 KOs) until he left his New England comfort zone to fight in Philadelphia, where he lost a ten-round majority decision to 27-3-1 hometown favorite Bobby Watts, but four years later Hagler knocked out 35-5-1 Watts in a rematch held in Portland, New Hampshire.

By then Hagler was a top-rated middleweight who had trouble finding name opponents to fight. The great Joe Frazier reportedly told him, "You have three strikes against you: you're black, you're a southpaw, and you're good." Hagler caught a break in 1976, when he took a fight on two weeks' notice on the road against another Philadelphia fighter, 32-3-1 Willie "The Worm" Monroe, who, ironically, was trained by Frazier. Hagler lost a ten-round unanimous decision (48-42, 47-44, 49-41) that was much closer than the final judges' scores may have indicated. Monroe unwisely gave him two rematches in 1977, which Hagler won by twelfth-round technical knockout and second-round knockout.

Hagler was cruising toward a seemingly inevitable world title shot, but it was still going to take time and patience, largely because Marvin was too much of a risk to fight. Hagler knocked out previously undefeated Mike Colbert (22-0), who suffered a broken jaw in the twelfth round, stopped Brit Kevin Finnegan twice, and then Hagler fought two more Philly fighters, 60-16-5 Benny Briscoe and 44-39-3 Willie Warren, who were decisioned in ten and retired after six rounds, respectively. The Hagler-Seales trilogy was completed in 1979 as Hagler knocked down Seales three times at the Boston Garden en route to an opening round stoppage.

World champions Rodrigo Valdez and then Hugo Corro refused to give Hagler a title shot. In 1979, Hagler finally got his first world title shot against WBC and WBA world middleweight champion Vito Antuofermo (45-3-1) at famed Caesars Palace in Las Vegas. Hagler, though, played it too close to vest, and Antuofermo retained his title belt due to a controversial fifteen-round draw (144-142, 141-145, 143-143) in which most observers felt Hagler had easily won.

Antuofermo lost his title to Alan Minter (38-6), so Hagler packed his bags and traveled to London to challenge the new local hero. Hagler didn't play it safe this fight, beating the game Minter into a bloody pulp, finally closing the show in the third. A riot broke loose at Wembley Arena. Minter had asked to be beat like a drum, claiming before the fight that "No black man is going to take my title." Hagler took his title and Minter's dignity, carving him up like a Thanksgiving turkey. Unfortunately, at least for Team Hagler, beer bottles and glasses rained down on them as police had to escort them back to the locker room from the ring.

After waiting so long to be in a world title fight, Hagler was determined to be a busy world champion, defending his crown often and seemingly everywhere. In 1981, Hagler knocked out previously undefeated Fulgencio Obelmejias (30-0) in the eighth-round at Boston Garden, 46-5-2 former world champion Antuofermo in a rematch that Vito's corner stopped before the start of the fourth, and 32-1-2 Mustafa Hamsho, who had beaten Wilfred Benitez, reached the eleventh round before succumbing in what had been a one-sided fight in Hagler's favor. Hagler became the first middleweight to earn a $1 million purse for his fight versus Hamsho.

William "Caveman" Lee (21-2) didn't make it through the first round. Obelmejias was eliminated in the fifth round of their rematch held in Italy. British challenger Tony Sibson (47-3-1) was stopped in the sixth. By then Hagler had become a regular on HBO PPV, and he obliterated 26-3 Wilford Scypion by way of a fourth-round

TKO in which he added the vacant IBF title to his WBA and WBA championships.

As the undisputed world middleweight king, Hagler closed out 1983 with a hard-fought victory over legendary Roberto Duran (77-4), who became the first title challenger to extend Hagler the full distance, after he had registered seven consecutive KO wins. Hagler likely showed Duran—who was the WBA Light Middleweight World Champion moving up to take on Hagler—too much respect as the Brockton fighter trailed on two cards with the third even after thirteen rounds. Despite a badly swollen left eye, Hagler answered the call and finished the last two rounds strong to win the fifteen-round decision (144-142, 144-143, 146-145).

Argentinian Juan Roldan (52-2-2) became the first to be credited with a knockdown of Hagler, which was clearly a slip early in the first round. Hagler took great offense and tried to brutalize Roldan in Las Vegas until the end mercifully came in the tenth round. This is the fight that gave Sugar Ray Leonard the idea that he could make a comeback and defeat a "slowing down" Hagler.

Hagler gave Hamsho a rematch, but the Syrian lasted only three rounds, frankly due to three headbutts Hamsho gave him. The normally under control Hagler was extremely angry, translating into a Hagler boxing blitzkrieg as he pounded Hamsho into submission.

Next came the incredible fight against 40-1 Thomas "Hitman" Hearns in what was simply billed "The Fight" at Caesars Palace. The April 15, 1985, showdown is still one of the most exciting and entertaining three-round fights in boxing history. The fighters charged to the center of the ring and Hearns, known as a lethal puncher, landed a powerful straight right to Hagler's chin. Amazingly, Hagler started walking through Hearns' punches, and Hagler suffered a cut on his head from an unintentional elbow or headbutt that, in typical Hagler fashion, did not even slow down the champion. Hearns, who had broken his right hand in the closing minute of the opening round, fought in reverse, attempting to move around the ring. He soon became cannon fodder for Hagler, who was incensed by the cut, especially after referee, Richard Steele, had the ringside physician examine Hagler's head at the beginning of the third. Feeling that the doctor may halt the action because of the bloody cut and award the victory to Hearns, Hagler charged the much taller Hearns and nailed him with an overhand right above Hearns' ear. Hearns wobbled, Hagler attacked, and the Detroit fighter was soon on the canvas. He rose at the count of eight but collapsed in Steele's arms as the bout was halted. A total of eight minutes, one second resulted in the 1985 Fight of the Year and round one of the 1985 Round of the Year.

"People talk about Tommy's right hand," Hagler later explained, "but the hardest punch I ever took was from my mother. Seriously, Tommy got through with a great right hand, but that was good because I wanted him to be confident with that shot. Our solution was to come under the straight punches, get inside, and go to work. It wasn't easy but the strategy was perfect. I was also cut in round one, maybe I hit my head on Tommy's cup, but I felt no pain. I knew that eventually I would wear him down and he belonged to me. I ate up his right hands like Pac-Man. I had prepared myself for battle and my body was like armor."

Olympic silver medalist and no. 1 contender John Mugabi (25-0) of Uganda was the lone fight Hagler had in 1986. It was delayed due to a back injury sustained by Hagler, whose critics were speculating age and attrition were finally catching up with the longtime champion. Making his twelfth consecutive world title defense, Hagler appeared to be slower and easier for Mugabi to hit. Hagler stood flat-footed, bashing instead of boxing Mugabi, but he eventually broke down a tiring Mugabi, closing the show in the eleventh round with a knockout.

Even Hagler's veteran promoter, Bob Arum, speculated that Hagler may retire instead of accepting the challenge to face 33-1 Sugar Ray Leonard, who was coming out of a three-year retirement, fighting only once in five years. Key pre-fight conditions were agreed upon that came back to haunt Hagler, who in return for receiving a larger share of the purse, agreed to fight in a larger ring, using ten-ounce gloves rather than eight ounces, a twelve-round scheduled fight instead of the traditional (at that time for a world title fight) fifteen. These three factors each favored Leonard on April 6, 1987, at Caesars Palace.

Hagler-Leonard was fought for Hagler's WBC and lineal titles. The WBA had stripped Hagler for fighting Leonard instead of its mandatory challenger Herol Graham, while the IBF refused to sanction the fight, declaring the title would be considered vacant if Leonard won. Hagler, who was a prohibitive favorite, chose to fight in an orthodox stance instead of his natural southpaw style, which proved to be a mistake as Leonard took the first two rounds. Hagler switched back to his southpaw stance in the third round and he did much better, and in the fifth round Leonard started showing signs of tiring. The challenger clinched so often that referee Steele issued thirty warnings for holding, although he did not penalize Leonard by docking him a single point. Hagler continued to press Leonard, who seemed to steal rounds, throwing a flurry of flashy punches in the final seconds of each round. Leonard was announced the winner by way of a disputed twelve-round split decision, but the judges' scores were all over the place: 115-113 Hagler, 115-113 Leonard, and somehow 118-110 for Leonard. A pool of ringside media favored Leonard, 14-9-8.

Hagler called for a rematch, but Leonard retired for his third time. A little more than a year later, Hagler announced his retirement from boxing, arguing that he had waited long enough for Leonard to grant a rematch. A month after Hagler retired, Leonard suddenly announced that he would return to fight WBC light heavyweight champion Donny Lalonde. In 1990, Leonard reportedly offered a $15 million rematch purse to Hagler, who had settled in Italy, but Marvin declined the offer. Hagler got married in Italy, where he lived and starred in some movies, most notably as Sgt. Jake Iron, who fought to save the rainforest against corporations.

Marvelous Marvin Hagler only lost three of his sixty-seven pro fights, never was stopped, and only floored once (even though that was clearly a slip), and one of the greatest boxers of all-time, arguably the no. 1 middleweight, right at the top of the 160-pounder mythical boxing mountain with Carlos Monzón.

ALL-NEW ENGLAND

Birth Name: Marvin Nathaniel Hagler
Nickname: Marvelous
Born: May 23, 1954, in Newark, New Jersey
Hometown: Brockton, Massachusetts
Death: March 13, 2021
Amateurs: 52-2 (43 KOs), 1973 National AAU champion and Most Outstanding Fighter of the tournament
Pro Record: 62-3-2 (52 KOs, 0 KOBY)
Pro Titles: Three-time world middleweight (September 27, 1980–March 21. 1987, September 27, 1980–April 6, 1987, May 27, 1983–April 6, 1987)
Pro Career: 1973–87
Height: 5' 9.5"
Reach: 75"
Stance: Southpaw
Division: Middleweight

World Title Fight Record: 13-1-1 (12 KOs)
Records vs. World Champions: 7-1-1 (6 KOs), defeated Alan Minter, Fulgencio Obelmejias (2), Vito Antuofermo, Roberto Duran,* Thomas Hearns,* John Mugabi; lost to Sugar Ray Leonard*; draw with Vito Antuofermo (* International Boxing HOF)

Manager: Goody and Pat Petronelli
Trainer: Goody and Pat Petronelli

Notes: International Boxing Hall of Fame, Class of 1993; held the highest knockout rate (78%) of undisputed world middleweight champion; 1983 and 1985 BWAA Fighter of the Year; 1983 and 1985 (shared with Donald Curry) *The Ring* Fighter of the Year; 1990 *Boxing Illustrated* Fighter of the Year; named third greatest middleweight of the twentieth century by Associated Press (AP)

No. 4

SANDY SADDLER

Willie Pep's Worst Nightmare

In his second professional fight, three-time, two-division world champion Sandy Saddler was knocked out by Jock Leslie, which proved to be a true outlier, because Saddler was never stopped again in his following 160 fights.

Saddler is best known for his four fights versus the great Willie Pep, in which Saddler won three, and he had a superlative 8-1 record in world title fights, losing only to Pep during his twelve-year pro career.

It all started in 1944 when Saddler won an eight-round unanimous decision against 30-7-3 Earl Roys in Hartford. Debuting in a scheduled eight-rounder against an opponent with thirty wins in forty fights were strong indications that Saddler was considered a very special fighter from the beginning. Two weeks later, he took three counts in the third round against Leslie, then retired on the stool for the lone stoppage of his glorious career.

Boston-native Saddler won his next fifteen fights before he lost in a six-round bout on points to 6-1 Lou Alter in Brooklyn, at once followed by a four-round draw with Alter only eight days later. And then Saddler won twenty-nine fights in a row until he dropped a ten-round unanimous decision to 16-4 Bobby McQuillar at Arena Gardens in Detroit. Later, in 1946, again in Detroit, Saddler lost to 53-13-10 Phil

Terranova, a former world champion, by way of a unanimous ten-round decision.

A sixteen-win skein was snapped in 1947 as 26-4-1 Jimmy Carter and Saddler fought to a ten-round majority draw at Griffith Stadium in Washington, DC. Saddler's unbeaten streak continued for four more fights until Saddler lost a ten-round split decision in a terrific fight to 28-7-3 Humberto Sierra in Minneapolis. Another streak, fourteen fights this time, was broken by 32-3 Chico Rosa in 1948, again by way of a ten-round split decision, in Honolulu.

Three added wins led to Saddler's initial world title fight, as well as his first match with defending world featherweight champion Pep, at Madison Square Garden. Pep entered the ring with an astonishing 134-1-1 record, while Saddler sported a not-too-shabby 85-6-2 mark. Saddler knocked out Pep, who was dropped and finished off in the third round.

Saddler-Pep II occurred on February 22, 1949, three months after Saddler had taken Pep's belt, and Pep regained the championship with a fifteen-round unanimous decision (10-5, 9-5, 9-5) at Madison Square Garden in *The Ring* magazine's 1949 Fight of the Year.

Saddler reeled off another long win streak, twenty-six, including statement victories against 42-3-1 Paddy DeMarco, 28-66 Orlando Zulueta (DEC10) for the vacant World Junior Lightweight Championship (this weight class's first champion in sixteen years), and 38-15-6 Lauro Salas (TKO9) in Saddler's first world junior lightweight title defense. Saddler's twenty-fourth straight win on this skein was against world featherweight champion Pep, who then had a 152-2-1 record. Pep was dropped in the third and unable to continue in the eighth round after suffering a separated shoulder in the seventh at Yankee Stadium in 1950.

A loss to 44-0-1 Del Flanagan in a non-title fight didn't slow down Saddler, who successfully defended his world junior lightweight title in a crazy fight that ended with 74-26-8 Diego Sosa out cold after two rounds. It was reported that Sosa had stepped on Saddler's shoes and brushed his hair over his eyes during clinches. Saddler responded with rabbit punches. They went down together, and Saddler managed to land a few shots during the scrum. Saddler rose at the count of eight,

Sosa didn't and was counted out. The Cuban fighter had the hometown crowd behind him in Havana, and thinking Sosa had been fouled, they rioted. The National Boxing Association (NBA) refused to recognize Saddler as its world junior lightweight champion any longer, ruling its champion could only hold one title at a time.

Saddler had an eighteen-win streak alive going to a rematch with 57-5-1 DeMarco, who won a ten-round split decision in Milwaukee. But in his next fight, Saddler rebounded with a successful 1951 world title defense win against 160-3-1 Pep, who retired after nine rounds in one of the dirtiest championship fights of all time. The New York Athletic Association revoked Pep's license and suspended Saddler.

Saddler lost three fights in a row immediately after his fourth fight with Pep. In order, to 60-5-1 DeMarco (DEC10), 39-1 George Araujo (DEC10), and 37-7-3 Armand Savoie (DQ3). In 1952, Saddler was drafted into the US Army and his world featherweight title was suspended for his two-year stint in military service. Saddler won five of six fights after being discharged. Saddler then lost a ten-round unanimous decision to future world champion Flash Elorde (29-8-2), which he avenged seven months later, stopping Elorde on cuts in the seventh round in another title defense.

In 1955, Saddler won another title defense by way of a fifteen-round unanimous decision against 63-50-5 Teddy Davis at Madison Square Garden in another notoriously dirty fight. Saddler didn't fight again for fourteen months, when he lost a ten-round unanimous decision to 29-2 Larry Boardman at the Boston Garden.

The relatively skinny Saddler, who was known to use every dirty trick in the book and maybe a few new underhanded maneuvers, retired as world featherweight champion in 1957, unfortunately due to a detached retina to his right eye, suffered six months earlier in a taxi accident.

If not for his "dirty fighting" reputation and four losses on the road by split decision, as well as a loss by disqualification, plus early retirement at the age of thirty-one, Sandy Saddler (145-16-2) may very well be ranked as no. 1 in New England instead of Pep, who lost three of four to his personal nightmare opponent.

ALL-NEW ENGLAND

Birth Name: Joseph Saddler
Nickname: Sandy
Born: June 23, 1926, in Boston, Massachusetts
Hometown: Boston, Massachusetts
Death: September 18, 2001
Pro Record: 145-16-2 (104 KOs, 1 KOBY)
Pro Titles: Two-time world featherweight champion (October 29, 1948–February 11, 1949 and September 8, 1950–January 21, 1957; world junior lightweight champion (December 6, 1949–September 8, 1950)
Pro Career: 1944–1956
Height: 5' 8.5"
Reach: 70"
Stance: Orthodox
Division: Featherweight

World Title Fight Record: 8-1 (6 KOs, 0 KOBY)
Records vs. World Champions: 9-4-1 (7 KOs, 0 KOBY), defeated Willie Pep (3),* Flash Elorde,* Paddy DeMarco (2), Lauro Salas (2), Joe Brown; lost to Willie Pep,* Flash Elorde,* Phil Terranova, Paddy DeMarco; draw with Jimmy Carter* (* International Boxing HOF)

Manager: Charlie Johnston
Trainer: Jimmy Brooks, Bert Briscoe

Notes: International Boxing Hall of Fame, Class of 1990; his nephew is hip-hop pioneer Grandmaster Flash (birth name Joseph Saddler); his cousin, Dick Sadler (used only one D in last name), trained George Foreman from pro debut to his loss to Muhammad Ali; Sandy and Archie Moore were Foreman's assistant trainers; became a trainer in New York City; died of dementia at the age of seventy-five; second greatest featherweight of the twentieth century by Associated Press (AP)

No. 5

SAM LANGFORD

"The Boston Tar Baby"
The Greatest Non-World Champion

The greatest boxer never to be world champion is unquestionably Sam "The Boston Tar Baby" Langford, who was a victim of racism in boxing during his entire twenty-four-year pro career, joining other leading "black" boxers in the early part of the twentieth century who rarely, if ever, received world title shots.

It is erroneously reported in places that Langford (178-29-38, 126 KOs) never fought for the world title, when in fact he fought fellow Boston-based, Canada-native black fighter "Barbados" Joe Walcott to a controversial draw in 1904 for the World Welterweight Championship.

Throughout his Hall of Fame career, Langford fought between lightweight and heavyweight, defeating a long list of Hall of Fame and/or world champions, which made his name as one of the greatest boxers of all time.

Born in Nova Scotia, Langford escaped from his abusive father and settled in Boston, where he worked as a janitor in a gym at Lennox Athletic Club, eventually learning how to box and becoming an amateur boxer. His first pro boxing match occurred at that same gym in 1902, resulting in a fifth-round knockout of Jack McVicker.

In his second year as a professional, Langford firmly established himself by outpointing the reigning world lightweight champion Joe

Gans (134-8-17) in a fifteen-round non-title fight. The first African American world champion in boxing, Gans went on to be recognized as one of the all-time greats and a Hall of Famer, and the two adversaries reportedly became good friends.

The only legitimate world title fight for Langford was in 1904, when he fought Walcott to a draw at Lake Massabesic Coliseum in Manchester, New Hampshire. Walcott retained his world title, but he was a bloody mess who was floored in the third round, while the larger Langford was practically unscratched after the action ended.

Langford's most memorable fights were primarily against other black fighters and future Hall of Famers such as Sam McVea (Langford's record in their rivalry: 6-2-7), Battling Jim Johnson (9-0-3), Joe Jeanette (8-2-4), George Godfrey and Henry Wills (2-14-2), and Joe Louis' future trainer, Jack Blackburn (1-0-4, 1 NC). Langford was a five-time world "colored" heavyweight champion, and most of his title fights were against the aforementioned black fighters.

In 1910, Langford won a six-round decision over Stanley Ketchell (48-5-4), who only eight months earlier had vacated his world middleweight championship, but a rumored rematch never materialized. A year later, Sam knocked out former world light heavyweight champion "Philadelphia" Jack O'Brien (147-13-25) in the fifth round of what had been a close encounter, after Langford nailed his opponent with a lethal left hook that signaled the end.

Langford, who reportedly was a trash-talker much like future world heavyweight champion Muhammad Ali, beat other top-notch fighters such as Young Peter Jackson, Fireman Jimmy Flynn, Tiger Flowers, Gunboat Smith, and Dixie Kid, among the more notables.

In a 1906 fight that likely best illustrated Langford's overall boxing talent, he lost a fifteen-round decision to legendary Jack Johnson in Chelsea, Massachusetts. Johnson must have learned an invaluable lesson, because he repeatedly refused to give Langford a rematch, alleging there wasn't sufficient money in another fight versus Langford. The "color barrier" that banned black fighters, ironically, continued through Johnson's reign from 1908 to 1915 as world heavyweight champion. When Johnson finally agreed to fight a black challenger, it was Battling

Jim Johnson rather than the more highly regarded Langford. And when Johnson lost the title in 1915 to Jess Willard, the latest on a long list of fighters dubbed the "Great White Hope," it would be another twenty-two years before another black heavyweight was given a world title shot: Joe Louis.

Langford also missed a lucrative fight against heavyweight boxing icon Jack Dempsey, who wouldn't fight Langford, not because of the color of his skin, rather as Dempsey wrote in his autobiography, "There was one man . . . I wouldn't fight because I knew he would flatten me. I wouldn't fight Sam Langford."

Not only is Sam Langford the greatest non-world champion in boxing history, but he may also be one of boxing's least known stars. If only Johnson had given him a rematch or Dempsey had given him an opportunity to fight, maybe more boxing media and fans would rightfully give Langford his just due.

ALL-NEW ENGLAND

Birth Name: Samuel Edgar Langford
Nickname: The Boston Tar Baby
Born: March 3, 1883, in Weymouth, Nova Scotia, Canada
Hometown: Boston, Massachusetts
Death: January 12, 1956
Amateurs: Amateur featherweight champion of Boston
Pro Record: 178-29-38 (126 KOs, 8 KOBY)
Pro Career: 1902–1926
Height: 5' 7.5"
Reach: 74"
Stance: Orthodox
Division: Heavyweight to lightweight

World Title Fight Record: 0-0-1
Records vs. World Champions: 6-1-2 (4 KOs), defeated George Godfrey,* Stanley Ketchell,* Joe Gans,* Philadelphia Jack O'Brien,* Dixie Kid* (twice), lost to Jack Johnson*; draw with Godfrey,* Joe Walcott (* International Boxing HOF)

Notes: International Boxing Hall of Fame, Class of 1990; left home in Canada to escape abuse; top ten in knockouts of all time with 126; named ninth heavyweight of the twentieth century by Associated Press (AP)

No. 6

JOHN L. SULLIVAN

"The Boston Strong Boy"
America's First Sports Idol

The "Roaring Twenties" were also known as America's golden age of sports, with superstars such as Babe Ruth and Jack Dempsey, who were bigger than life. But America's first sports idol was the original world heavyweight champion John L. Sullivan, one of the world's highest paid athletes of his era.

The infamous Boston brawler, sporting his trademark handlebar moustache, was the son of Irish immigrants who wanted their son to be a Roman Catholic priest. But he had plans to be a professional baseball player, leaving Boston College in 1875 to purse his dreams on the diamond.

But Sullivan had fighting in his veins, and as a teenager he fought in Boston ballrooms, loudly claiming that he "could lick any SOB in the house." He went on to become the link between bare knuckles and glove fighting. Among the many credits he's received is his fights launched boxing coverage in newspapers, setting the template for covering prizefights in the media.

The wild Irish American fighter was arrested numerous times as a youth for fighting in states where it was banned. He traveled on exhibition tours, boldly offering people money to fight him, and he reportedly had nearly 500 fights during his career. In 1883–84, Sullivan embarked on a cross-country tour with five other boxers. They were supposed to have 195 fights in 136 different cities and towns during a 238-day span. Always a promoter at heart, Sullivan challenged anybody to fight him under the Queensbury Rules for $250, knocking out eleven men.

Sullivan's first recorded pro fight was March 13, 1879, in Boston, when he knocked out Jack Curley. The first six of Sullivan's pro career matches were in Boston, after which he started touring the United States to fight in Cincinnati, New York City, Yonkers (NY), Philadelphia, Chicago, Mississippi City and Richburg (MS), Rochester (NH), Brooklyn, Buffalo, Fort Wayne (IN), Tacoma (WA), McKeesport (PA), East St. Louis (IL), Saint Paul (MN), Davenport (IA), Butte (MT), Astoria (OR), Seattle, San Francisco, Galveston (TX), Hot Springs (AK), Memphis, Nashville, and Pittsburgh. "The Boston Strong Boy" also fought in Chantilly, France; Cardiff, Wales; Toronto and Victoria, Canada,

In 1882, Sullivan stopped Ireland's Paddy Ryan in round nine to become the American bare-knuckle heavyweight champion. Depending on what records you believe, Sullivan captured the inaugural world heavyweight title in 1885, overcoming a first-round knockdown to win a decision against American 15-0-2 Dominick McCaffrey in Cincinnati. Or in 1989, when he knocked out Somerville (MA) heavyweight Jake Kilrain in the seventy-fifth round of a scheduled eighty-round fight in Richburg, Mississippi, even though that was billed as a world bare-knuckle fight.

The Sullivan-Kilrain fight was the last bare-knuckle heavyweight title fight, as well as one of the greatest sporting events, receiving national press coverage in the US. It appeared that John L. was going to lose, especially after he vomited, but a revitalized Sullivan roared back, and Kilrain's corner threw in the towel after the seventy-fifth round.

Sullivan didn't fight again for four years in what turned out to be his final fight in 1892, against 8-0-2 James J. Corbett, who was the complete opposite of Sullivan style-wise, a boxer compared to slugger Sullivan. Corbett outboxed an out-of-shape Sullivan, breaking down the Irish American hero on his way to a twenty-first round knockout in New Orleans to become world heavyweight champion.

Because today's official boxing record keeper, BoxRec, doesn't acknowledge fights under London Prize Ring rules, Sullivan retired with a 38-1-1 (32 KOs), rather than 47-1-2. The man who was the first swagger king of sports later became an actor.

John L. Sullivan, despite criticism that he refused to fight any black boxers, is remembered as the first lineal world heavyweight champion and the connection between bare knuckles and gloved fighting.

ALL-NEW ENGLAND

Birth Name: John Lawrence Sullivan
Nickname: The Boston Strong Boy
Born: October 15, 1858, in Roxbury, Massachusetts
Hometown: Roxbury, Massachusetts
Death: February 2, 1918
Pro Record: 38-1-1 (32 KOs, 1 KOBY)
Pro Titles: World heavyweight (August 29, 1885–September 7, 1892)
Pro Career: 1879–92
Height: 5' 10.5"
Reach: 74"
Stance: Orthodox
Division: Heavyweight

World Title Fight Record: 1-1 (1 KOBY)
Records vs. World Champions: 0-1 lost to James J. Corbett*

Manager: Billy Madden
Trainer: William Muldoon, Prof. Jim Kelly

Notes: International Boxing Hall of Fame, Class of 1990; claimed the only man to knock him down in the ring was Jack Hogan; died at the age of sixty from a heart attack, and when he was buried, the ground was frozen so hard that dynamite had to be used; Kilrain, who served as a pallbearer, said, "Old John L. would have approved."

No. 7

VINNY PAZIENZA

"Pazmanian Devil"
Boxing's Greatest Comeback

Forget about Muhammad Ali, "Sugar" Ray Robinson, "Sugar" Ray Leonard, or George Foreman, Vinny Pazienza made the greatest comeback in boxing history, probably in all of sports. And it had nothing to do with coming back to fight at an advanced age. He returned to the ring thirteen months after suffering a broken neck in a car accident to eventually become world champion once again.

"The more I talk about it," Pazienza offered, "I realize how lucky I really was. I could have easily ended up in a wheelchair like a lot of people. I got very lucky. I worked hard, but thank God, I was so lucky."

Pazienza also revealed that there is a documentary in the process of being filmed about him, *The Greatest Comeback in Sports History*, supported by Dana White and possibly being filmed by Tom Brady's group.

The charismatic Italian American boxer from Cranston, Rhode Island, was a boxing "rock star" during the eighties and nineties, rarely seen in public without a beautiful woman or two on his arm (usually exotic dancers or porn stars), and a special guest on high profile television shows and movies. Also known as a notorious gambler, Pazienza (50-10, 30 KOs) played the bright spotlight to his advantage and built a passionate worldwide fan base.

"So much shit went down with me," Paz admitted. "I did a little bit of everything, and things happened to me. I remember listening to Howard Stern one day and he had porn star Tyler Faith on as a guest. He kept saying she was so nice and smart, and asked her why she got into porn. She said that she always wanted to be in porn. I called up the show and said that little bitch, I told her to get into porn. Howard went back on the air and said to her, wait a minute, I just got a call. You didn't tell me you dated world champion fighter Vinny Paz from Providence."

Vinny was a highly decorated amateur boxer on Team USA. He befriended a younger, rather shy teammate by the name of Mike Tyson.

"I knew Tyson was an animal, a beast. I saw it in his face even back then. He was always reading. We were on the USA Olympic Team in 1982. I remember Tyson sparring (Tyrone) Biggs. We traveled together to Yugoslavia, Russia, Ireland, and Scandinavia. I was arrested in Russia. I was the East Coast wise guy. In Russia, I sold hats and T-shirts for rubles. The other fighters and coach Pat Nappi gave me shirts to sell for them. I was thrown in jail. A guy there asked me if I as Vinny Pazienza. He said I didn't belong there, and he took me back to where I was staying. If it wasn't for him, I'd still be there, and nobody would know."

Paz eventually outgrew New England.

"It was cool being a New England fighter," Pazienza said. "I thought it was a little different, harder to make it out of here. I thought I was a combination of Pep, Marciano, and Ali. Those three guys wrapped up what I wanted to do. I couldn't do much more than I did. I had a lot of good fights in New England. My fight with Glenwood Brown (1988 at Foxwoods) was great. Fighting in front of my fans was great. We sold out the Providence Civic Center (16,000 fans in 1986). It was electric, unbelievable, a madhouse. I was 17-1. But I never felt like a New England. I was Vinny Paz, that's it. I didn't fight like I was a New England or California fighter. I had my own style and did what I did. I mostly trained in Rhode Island, but I also trained in New Hampshire. I stayed in Atlantic City a lot to train for big fights I had there. My favorite place is Vegas. I still go there all the time."

On a side note, I worked the Mike Tyson World Comeback Tour and at a press conference in Youngstown, Ohio, for the first (and only) Tyson fight. I found myself alone with Tyson sitting at the dais. I desperately tried to not stare at his face tattoo, and blurted out, "Hello from a mutual friend, Vinny Paz." Tyson slowly shook his head, smiled, and said, "Vinny Paz . . . now that's one crazy motherfucker." I've repeated this story countless times, especially when Vinny wanted me to tell the story. He felt it was the highest honor, saying, "Imagine, Mike Tyson thinks I'm a crazy motherfucker!"

Pazienza legally changed his last name to Paz in 2000. "I changed my name because I wanted to do something different in 2000," Paz explained. "I was hanging with Larry Holmes, and he couldn't pronounce Pazienza. I finally said to him, just call me Paz, and I changed my name because of him."

Paz was always wired from the opening bell, entertaining the crowd with his colorful in-ring antics. He made his pro debut on May 26, 1983, in Atlantic City, knocking out Alfredo Rivera in the fourth round. Vinny won his first fifteen pro fights, and after suffering a loss by fifth-round TKO to 14-3 Abdelkader Marbi, he went on a tear that made him an East Coast monster, winning eight in a row to improve to 22-1. During this stretch he defeated 19-2 Jeff Bumpus (DEC10) and 22-6 Melvin Paul (TKO2) in Atlantic City, as well as 15-2-3 Joe Frazier Jr. (TKO7), 29-2 former world champion Harry Arroyo (DEC10), 31-03 Nelson Bolanos (TKO6), and 31-5 Roberto Elizondo (DEC15) in Providence, Rhode Island.

In Providence, on June 7, 1987, Pazienza got his first world title shot against undefeated IBF lightweight world champion Greg Haugen. Pazienza was crowned after winning a fifteen-round unanimous decision on scores of 144-141 three times. There was a great deal of animosity between Pazienza and Haugen, to say the least, increasing exponentially through their trilogy. Pazienza-Haugen II was held February 6, 1988, again in Providence, but Haugen regained the IBF belt by winning a unanimous decision (147-138 X2, 145-140) in the last fifteen-round match in boxing.

Pazienza would soon move up to super lightweight, unsuccessfully challenging WBC super lightweight world champion Roger Mayweather (33-5), who won a twelve-round unanimous decision (118-108, 117-110 X 2) at Caesars Palace in Las Vegas. In 1999, Pazienza challenged WBO super lightweight world champion and future Hall of Fame boxer 36-0 Hector Camacho, losing a twelve-round unanimous decision (116-117, 112-115, 109-119) in Atlantic City.

"Hector Camacho was unbelievable," Paz emphatically stated. "He was super fast and hard to fight. I couldn't get in on him to catch him, and I was the fastest white guy in the game. When Camacho fought me, he was at the top of his game. He was a good puncher, too. I went into the fight hoping I could land a bomb. I just couldn't do it."

The third match in his trilogy with Haugen, now 25-2, was held during the summer of 1990 in Atlantic City, and Pazienza took the edge in the series, winning a ten-round unanimous decision (98-92, 97-93, 96-94) to move him into contention for another world title.

"I hate that little prick"—Paz still gets fired up talking about Haugen—"and that was from day one. He's a dick! One of my favorite fights was our third when I won the second fight."

In Sacramento, California, Pazienza challenged WBA world super lightweight champion Loreto Garza (27-1-1), who stopped Pazienza in the eleventh round. Pazienza won the United States Boxing Association (USBA) super welterweight title in his next fight, taking a twelve-round unanimous decision from 20-4-1 Ron Amundson, positioning the popular pugilist for another world title shot on October 1, 1991, in Providence, versus unbeaten defending champion Gilbert Dele (29-0-1), knocking him out in the twelfth and final round in a close fight he led going into the twelfth (107-104, 107-102, 106-106). Pazienza became only the second fighter to capture both the world lightweight and junior middleweight championships.

Pazienza, though, had to relinquish his title belt because of the aforementioned car accident, in which he broke his neck and was told to never mind fighting again, he may never walk. Pazienza, however, is a different type of fighter. Going against doctors' orders, Pazienza secretly started working out, wearing a halo screwed into his skull for six months. Thirteen months after suffering his injury, Pazienza triumphantly returned to the ring at what would become his second home, Foxwoods Resort Casino (only a forty-five-minute drive from his Cranston home), where he defeated 36-14-2 Luis Santana by way of a shutout performance, winning each round for a ten-round unanimous decision (100-90, 100-88, 100-89).

"You gotta have balls," Paz forcefully talked about coming back from a broken neck to win the world title again. "You don't do anything in life without balls. I was in a weird situation talking about coming back on national TV and saying this (broken neck) wasn't the end. Then I'd go home and look in the mirror with my halo screwed into my skull and ask myself why I was doing this. Why would I do this because I could have ended up in a wheelchair? I always had a motto: make it happen or die trying."

Less than four months later, Paz returned to Foxwoods to meet 31-7 veteran Brett Lally, who was unable to continue after six rounds.

Successive victories against another former world champion: 41-3 Lloyd Honeyghan TKO10), Marvin Hagler's half-brother 37-92 Robbie Sims (DEC10), 22-5 Dan Sherry (KO11) for the International Boxing Organization (IBO) world super middleweight title, 22-7-2 Jacques LeBlanc (DEC10), living legend (92-9) Robert Duran (DEC12) for the International Boxing Council (IBC) super middleweight championship, 33-13 Rafael Williams, and Duran (DEC12) again in an IBC defense.

"Duran was a big puncher," Paz remembered. "I'm glad I didn't fight him when he was 25 instead of (jokingly) 95. He still had power. He walked me out for my 50th win."

Undefeated IBF super middleweight world champion Roy Jones (28-0), who went on to win the world heavyweight title, outclassed the significantly smaller Pazienza, who lasted until the sixth round, in which he was decked three times.

"How did I fight the (future) heavyweight champion of the world when I was only 5' 7" on a good hair day," Pazienza rhetorically asked. "He was the greatest pound-for-pound fighter at that time as a super middleweight. He was tremendously fast like Camacho. After he beat me, he went on to beat John Ruiz to become the heavyweight champion of the world. He should have stayed there because he could have beaten a lot of the top heavyweights."

In a match dripping with pure hate (Paz reportedly sent Rosenblatt's mother a dozen black roses with a note saying Paz was sorry he had to kill her son) between New England fighters, Pazienza handed 28-0 World Boxing Union (WBU) Dana Rosenblatt, who was pounded into submission until the final curtain call in the fourth round. In 1997, Pazienza lost a twelve-round unanimous decision to WBC international super middleweight champion Herol Graham (47-5) in London. The resilient Pazienza bounced back with five solid wins in a row before he lost a twelve-round split decision (115-112, 113-114, 113-115) at Foxwoods to Rosenblatt for the vacant IBO super middleweight strap.

Three wins followed for Pazienza, who in 2002 challenged WBC world super middleweight title holder Eric Lucas (34-4-3), the winner of a decisive twelve-round unanimous decision 117-112, 119-110, 117-111) in Pazienza's final world title shot.

Two years later and sporting a 49-10 pro record, Pazienza vowed to win his fiftieth career fight and retire. His opponent on March 27, 2004, at Foxwoods, was 39-5 Tocker Pudwill, who started strong to take the early advantage, but a bloodied Paz finished strong to win a ten-round unanimous decision (96-93, 96-95 X 2).

Vinny Pazienza's remarkable comeback from a broken neck to become world champion resulted in him being named by *The Ring* magazine as the Comeback of the Year award winner, and his inspirational story was made into a 2016 film, *Bleed for This*, starring Miles Teller as Paz.

"I was the Providence hometown team for many years," Paz concluded. "I would fight anybody, anywhere, as long as the money was right. I'm so lucky God gave me a little extra. I'm so lucky. I know guys who had my 60 pro and more than 100 amateur fights who are shot today."

ALL-NEW ENGLAND

Birth Name:	Vincent Pazienza
Nickname:	Pazmanian Devil
Born:	December 16, 1962, in Cranston, Rhode Island
Hometown:	Cranston, Rhode Island
Amateurs:	100-12, 1982 National Sports Festival champion
Pro Record:	50-10 (30 KOs, 3 KOBY)
Pro Titles:	IBF world lightweight champion (June 7, 1987–February 6, 1988). WBA world super welterweight champion October 1, 1991)
Pro Career:	1983–2004
Height:	5' 7.5"
Reach:	70.5"
Stance:	Orthodox
Division:	Lightweight-super middleweight

World Title Fight Record: 2-6 (1 KO. 2 KOBYs)

Records vs. World Champions: 8-7 (3 KOs, 2 KOBYs), defeated Harry Arroyo, Greg Haugen (2), Gilbert Dele, Lloyd Honeyghan, Roberto Duran (2),* Luis Santana; lost to Greg Haugen, Roger Mayweather, Hector Camacho,* Loreto Garza, Roy Jones Jr., Aaron Davis, Eric Lucas (* International Boxing HOF)

Manager:	Lou Duva
Trainer:	Lou Duva and Kevin Rooney

Notes: In 2002, inducted into National Italian American Hall of Fame; the book *Fight or Die: The Vinny Paz Story* was written by Tommy Jon Caduto

No. 8

TONY DEMARCO

"Boston Bomber"
Short Reign, Long Life

Although his world title reign was brief (two months, nine days), Tony "Boston Bomber" DeMarco (58-12-1 33 KOs) defeated five world champions, including Hall of Famer Kid Gavilan, during his fourteen-year professional career, in addition to having a Hall of Fame career fighting the top welterweights in the world during the fifties.

The son of Sicilian immigrants who settled in the predominately Italian neighborhood of Boston, the North End, where the old Boston Garden stood (and TD Garden stands) and DeMarco is still beloved as "their" champ and a significant part of Boston's Italian American history, honored by the renaming of a street to "Tony DeMarco Way," as well as the erection of a statue of him.

Because pro boxers needed to be eighteen, sixteen-year-old Leonardo Liotta used the birth certificate of Tony DeMarco, and thus the story of the "Boston Bomber" started with his October 21, 1948, first-round knockout of Meteor Jones at the Boston Garden. Fighting exclusively in New England through late 1951, mostly Boston, DeMarco then started fighting in New York City, Newark, New Jersey, and even Montreal.

In 1953, DeMarco's career took off as he ripped off a seventeen-fight unbeaten streak, posting sixteen wins—ten by KO—and one draw. During this run he defeated solid opponents such as 55-34-4

Pat Demers (TKO6) and 70-27-5 Terry Young; took a ten-round split decision from former world champion 65-10-2) Paddy DeMarco, adding victories against 88-12-4 Johnny Cesario (DEC10), 52-5-12 George Araujo (TKO9) at Fenway Park, and then a ten-round with another former World Champion, 76-17-8 Jimmy Carter.

The highlight of DeMarco's career wasn't an April Fool's joke although coming on April 1, 1955, appropriately at Boston Garden, when he took out 46-3-2 defending world welterweight champion Jimmy Saxton (46-3-2) in the fourteenth round to become world champion. The celebration barely ended before DeMarco made his first and only world title defense at War Memorial Stadium in Buffalo against top contender and local favorite Carmen Basilio (44-11-7). It was a real war as the fighters took turns pounding each other. Basilio easily led on the judges' scorecard (8-2, 8-3, 7-4) going into the fatal twelfth round, when Basilio put DeMarco's lights out to take the world title belt.

DeMarco needed to regroup three months later, stopping 63-4-1 Chicco Vejar in the tenth round of their world welterweight title eliminator at Boston Garden.

Basilio-DeMarco was so exciting that their rematch was tremendously anticipated. The difference this time, however, was that the fight was held in DeMarco's backyard, Boston Garden. The fight was similar to their first confrontation as Basilio wore down DeMarco, who nearly won the belt back when his left hook had Basilio out on his feet. Unable to take advantage of this swing of momentum, Basilio went on to defend his title with a twelfth round stoppage. Named *The Ring* magazine's Fight of the Year, many boxing aficionados believe it was the greatest welterweight fight of all time.

Undeterred by his world title fight losses to Basilio, DeMarco knocked out 31-14-6 Wallace Bud Smith, decisioned 52-7-2 Arthur Presley and 50-3 Vince Martinez in a pair of ten-round bouts. Next was a Boston Garden showdown against immortal Kid Gavilan (104-21-5), in which DeMarco won a ten-round unanimous decision.

DeMarco then fought a trilogy with 40-6-1 Gasper Ortega, losing two ten-round split decisions at Madison Square Garden before he won a ten-round unanimous decision at Boston Garden. In 1957, DeMarco lost to 45-17-1 Virgil Atkins in back to back bouts at the Boston Garden for the Massachusetts version of the World Welterweight Championship because Basilio had moved up to middleweight. DeMarco was down six times in the first match, dropping Atkins in the twelfth, but the fight was dead even going into what turned out to be the final round (125-120, 123-123, 123-123). Prospects looked brighter for DeMarco in the rematch when he floored Atkins in the fourth round and he led decisively (9-2, 6-3, 5-4) going into the twelfth round. DeMarco was running out of gas though, having been dropped in the eighth, eleventh, and finally the twelfth round to end the fight.

The bloom was off the rose, so to speak, at this point for DeMarco, who had given and received so much damage during his highlight-film career. In his second to last fight, Tony knocked out yet another former world champion, 51-20-6 Don Jordan, in the second round. DeMarco hung up his gloves for good after winning a ten-round decision from 32-10-2 Stefan Redl at Boston Garden on February 6, 1962.

Fearless, ferocious, and relentless, Tony DeMarco's world title reign may have been short, but he was fondly remembered by boxing fans wherever he traveled, sitting at ringside for most New England-based boxing events for much of his later years until his passing in 2021 as the second oldest living world champion at that time.

He was finally selected to the International Boxing Hall of Fame in the Class of 2019. However, due to COVID restrictions cancelling back to back induction ceremonies, he was inducted posthumously in 2022.

ALL-NEW ENGLAND

Birth Name: Leo Liotta
Nickname: Boston Bomber
Born: January 14, 1932, in Boston, Massachusetts
Hometown: Boston, Massachusetts
Death: October 11, 2021
Pro Record: 58-12-1 (33 KOs, 7 KOBY)
Pro Titles: World welterweight champion (April 1, 1955–June 10, 1955)
Pro Career: 1948–52
Height: 5' 5"
Stance: Orthodox
Division: Welterweight

World Title Fight Record: 1-4 (1 KO, 4 KOBY)
Records vs. World Champions: 5-5-1 (3 KOs, 5 KOBY), defeated Paddy DeMarco, Johnny Saxton, Wallace Bud Smith, Kid Gavilan,* Don Jordan; lost to Carmen Basilio (2),* Virgil Atkins (2), Denny Moyer

Managers: Coogie McFarland, Angelo Pucci, Bobby Agripino
Trainers: Sammy Fuller, Frankie Waters

Notes: International Boxing Hall of Fame, Class of 2019; he was the second oldest living world champion at the age of eighty-eight when he passed away in 2021; inducted into the National Italian American Sports Hall of Fame; DeMarco's 1954 fight vs. Araujo was the last held at famed Fenway Park; 27-0 Rocky Marciano knocked out 22-11-7 Gino Buonvino on the same card as DeMarco's first-round TKO of 12-9 Roger Ringuette at Braves Field in Boston

No. 9

JACK SHARKEY

"Boston Gob"
Al Capone and Controversy Followed Sailor

Lost in the shadows of heavyweight stars from his era such as Jack Dempsey and Joe Louis, Jack "Boston Gob" Sharkey was followed throughout his pro boxing career by controversy, both good and bad, and he attracted famous fans as world heavyweight champion.

Born in Binghamton, New York, Sharkey moved to Boston as a child with his Lithuanian immigrant parents, where he later unsuccessfully tried several times to enlist in the US Navy because he was underage. He was unable to enlist until after World War I, when he was eighteen, and he was encouraged by his shipmates to box. During a 1924 return to port in Boston, he made his pro debut, knocking out Billy Muldoon at Mechanics Building. And before his discharge a month later, Jack won his second pro fight against Pat Hance by disqualification in round two.

At this point Sharkey took his boxing name instead of using his birth name, Joseph Zukauskas, combining the names of his two idols, Jack Dempsey and Tom Sharkey. Sharkey's first two years as a prizefighter drew mixed reviews, largely because he fought much more experienced opponents such as 64-18-5 Charley Weinert and 26-4-7 Bud Gorman. Sharkey registered solid victories over 51-8-2 Jack Renault (PTS10) and 16-1 Jim Maloney (DQ9), who dropped Sharkey five times before being disqualified for allegedly hitting Sharkey below the belt.

Sharkey won his rematch with Gordon, again on a controversial disqualification for low blows, which had started to become a questionable trend for the "Boston Gob." In mid-1926, Jack reversed the outcome of his first match with Gorman, winning a ten-round unanimous decision at Braves Field in Boston.

An impressive win in ten rounds on points against 30-10-1 George Godfrey opened the door for Sharkey to face another top "colored" boxer and future Hall of Famer, 85-7-7 Harry Wills (who most top-ranked heavyweights avoided like the plague), at Ebbets Field in Brooklyn. Sharkey surprisingly handled Wills, who was disqualified in the thirteenth round for striking Sharkey with an illegal backhand, marking Wills' first loss in four years, putting Sharkey in line for a world title shot against Gene Tunney.

Sharkey kept his arduous march on track for his first world title shot, stopping 57-39-7 Homer Smith in the seventh round, former world light heavyweight champion Mike McTigue (100-29-10) in the twelfth at Madison Square Garden, and 27-3 Maloney again in the fifth. Sharkey had earned a shot in a world heavyweight title eliminator against his idol 58-6-9 Dempsey on July 21, 1927, at Yankee Stadium. There were world title fight implications because the winner would become Tunney's mandatory challenger.

Cruising through six dominant rounds, Sharkey claimed he was hit with a low blow in the seventh round that, truthfully, appeared to have struck his midsection. Sharkey turned to complain to the referee, when he suddenly went down hard from a brutal Dempsey left hook. Sharkey stayed down, moaning and grabbing his groin area, but referee Jack O'Sullivan refused to allow it and counted out Sharkey. Dempsey's sudden KO victory announcement electrified the pro-Dempsey crowd, who had believed their hero and then former world heavyweight champion was going to lose the fight and opportunity to fight Tunney again for the world title. Loss or not, Sharkey had proven himself by getting the best of Dempsey; that is, right up until the fatal ending.

In 1928 at MSG, Sharkey fought a twelve-round split draw at MSG with former heavyweight contender Tom Heeney (31-8-4), and he lost a twelve-round split decision to 44-20-7 Johnny Risko.

An opening round knockout of future Hall of Famer Jack Delaney (71-20-1), also at MSG, put Sharkey back on the right course.

His reward was a slot in a heavyweight tournament to succeed Tunney, the retiring world heavyweight champion (promoted by legendary Tex Rickard), against future Hall of Famer Young Stribling (214-10-17), at Flamingo Park in Miami. Rickard suddenly passed away and the tournament, including Sharkey vs. Stribling, was in serious jeopardy. Dempsey, who was very close to Rickard, was appointed as Rickard's replacement. The heavyweight eliminator, won by Sharkey on points, attracted 40,000 fans and 423 media members, setting up a South record gate of $405,000, which lasted until Clay vs. Liston I in 1964.

Later, in 1929, Sharkey faced former two-time world champion and future Hall of Famer 92-14-8 Tommy Loughran before 45,000 at Yankee Stadium. Sharkey knocked out Loughran in the third round to capture the American heavyweight title, putting him in line for a match with Max Schmeling. First, though, Jack fought a fellow sailor, 64-10-4 Phil Scott, who had joined the British Navy at the age of fifteen to fight in World War I, and he later worked as a detective for two years at Scotland Yard. The Bostonian stopped Scott in the third round, when referee Lou Magnolia refused Scott's claim that he was fouled.

Sharkey, unfortunately, became a dubious part of boxing history in his first world title fight on June 12, 1997, at Yankee Stadium, when he became the first boxer to be disqualified in a world championship fight since Joe Goss in 1876. Considerably more experienced than his German foe, 42-4-3 Schmeling, Sharkey was disqualified in the fourth round for striking Schmeling below the belt.

Unfazed and more determined than ever, Sharkey relentlessly continued his mission to become heavyweight champion of the world, returning to action in late December to take on former two-division world champion Mickey Walker (112-16-2), who was moving up in weight to fight Sharkey. The two put on quite a show at Ebbets Field, with Sharkey outweighing his game opponent by nearly thirty pounds. They fought to a draw despite Sharkey recording the lone knockdown of the fight, and Jack moved on to fight 6' 5", 261-pound Primo Carnera

(48-3) in front of 30,000 people for the American heavyweight title. Sharkey outboxed and outclassed the Italian Giant, flooring him in the fourth round to win the fifteen-round match on points and secure the Schmeling rematch.

Schmeling (44-4-3) entered the ring on June 21, 1931, as the defending NBA and NYSAC world heavyweight champion, but Sharkey left with the world title belts after he won a fifteen-round split decision at Madison Square Garden Bowl. Many fans were upset with the debatable decision (8-7, 7-3, 5-10), chanting cries of robbery when the outcome was announced. The rubber match of their potential trilogy failed to materialize because Schmeling lost to explosive puncher Max Baer in 1933.

With the fame that went along with being world heavyweight champion (arguably the most coveted individual title in sports at that time), one of Sharkey's strongest supporters was infamous gangster Al Capone, who attended Sharkey's fights in New York City and Chicago, and owned a mansion in Palm Island, Florida, near Sharkey's training camp. On one occasion, Capone sent a case of beer during prohibition to the Boston gym where Sharkey trained, with a note saying he couldn't attend his upcoming fight and wishing him well. Athletes, movie stars, and other celebrities liked to hang with The Champ, and many visited him at his training camp.

Reportedly under pressure from the mob to fight Carnera, Sharkey defended his title for the first and last time, suspiciously knocked out in the sixth round at Madison Square Garden Bowl on June 19, 1933. Sharkey was having his way with Carnera, deftly using his speed and skill advantages, until he was caught with a right uppercut right on the button that sent him to never- never land in the sixth round. Many in the press shouted "fix," but Sharkey denied accusations to his dying days. Sharkey became the first world heavyweight champion to win and lose the title to European fighters, respectively Schmeling and Carnera—only the third and fourth world heavyweight champions from Europe at that time.

Sharkey's career went downhill relatively fast after his world title loss to Carnera, dropping a fifteen-round unanimous decision to 46-23-4

King Levinsky in Chicago, then he suffered a fifteen-round split decision loss to Loughran (110-23-8) in their 1933 rematch in Philadelphia. Jack returned for his first fight in two years on a controversial second-round knockout of 50-34-6 Unknown Winston in late 1935 at Boston Garden. Talk about a "fix" led right up to the fight. Sharkey knocked out Winston in the first round on two questionable blows that outraged fans who surrounded the ring as they shouted insults. The referee unsuccessfully spoke to the crowd, claiming Winston had given his best, but Sharkey suggested that they start the fight all over again, which was eventually allowed after a few minutes of discussion between officials. Sharkey decked Winston twice in the second round, the last proved to be the final blow in their "fight."

In 1936. Sharkey lost a ten-round decision and fought a ten-round draw in two fights with 69-10-6 Tony Shucco, followed by a win via a ten-round unanimous decision over 17-1-3 Phil Brubaker at Fenway Park. Sharkey overcame a first-round knockdown and a wicked gash over his left eye in the sixth round.

Sharkey's final fight of his twelve-year pro career unceremoniously concluded on August 18, 1936, at Yankee Stadium, when Jack was used as a name opponent for a rising star, Joe Louis (24-1), who floored Sharkey four times, the last resulting in a third-round knockout. Sharkey had made history once again as the only man to face all-time greats Dempsey and Louis.

Known as a gifted boxer who never consistently put it all together, sadly, Jack Sharkey is perhaps best remembered for being involved in so many controversial fights, some of which he won, others he lost.

ALL-NEW ENGLAND

Birth Name: Joseph Paul Zukauskas
Nickname: Boston Gob
Born: October 6, 1902, in Binghamton, New York
Hometown: Boston, Massachusetts
Death: August 17, 1994
Pro Record: 37-13-3 (13 KOs, 4 KOBY)
Pro Titles: World heavyweight champion (June 21, 1932–June 29, 1933)
Pro Career: 1924–1936
Reach: 76"
Stance: Orthodox
Division: Heavyweight

World Title Fight Record: 1-3 (0 KOs, 1 KOBY)
Records vs. World Champions: 4-5-1 (1 KO, 1 KOBY), defeated Max Schmeling,* Tommy Loughran,* Mike McTigue, Primo Carnera; lost to Max Schmeling,* Jack Dempsey,* Joe Louis,* Tommy Loughran,* Primo Carnera; draw with Mickey Walker* (* International Boxing HOF)

Manager: John Buckley
Trainer: Al Lacy, Tony Palazzolo

Notes: International Boxing Hall of Fame, Class of 1994; son of Lithuanian immigrants; fought in some unusual, famous venues known for hosting other sports: Fenway Park, Braves Field, and Boston Garden in Boston; Madison Square Garden, Yankees Stadium, and Ebbets Field in New York City; and Flamingo Park in Miami; only man to fight Jack Dempsey and Joe Louis; after he retired as a boxer, he owned a Boston bar and pro refereed boxing matches, including a pair between Archie Moore and Yvon Durelle; oldest living world heavyweight champion when he died in 1994 at the age of ninety-two in Epping, New Hampshire

No. 10

PAUL PENDER

Sugar Ray Robinson's Kryptonite

Two-time world middleweight champion Paul Pender made his boxing bones, so to speak, by beating arguably the greatest boxer of all-time, Sugar Ray Robinson, in not one but two world title fights in the early 1960's.

A star high school football player in his hometown of Brookline, Massachusetts, which borders Boston, talented enough to be recruited and offered scholarships by Michigan State and Penn State, Pender decided to pass on football to become a prizefighter, but he did study politics for a few years at Staley College in Brookline.

Pender, who was known as a cerebral boxer with a very high boxing IQ, was a New England champion as an amateur, who turned pro in 1949 in Boston, where he knocked out Paul Williams in the first round. Pender went unbeaten through his first twenty-one pro fights, the only blemish on his record a ten-round draw with 41-16-2 Bill Daley in 1949. After getting stopped in 1951 by Gene Hairston and the following year by Jimmy Beau in the fifth, Pender moved away from boxing and joined the US Marines, where he was a boxing coach.

After being out of boxing for 2.5 years, Pender returned to the ring in 1954 with a ten-round unanimous decision against 45-5-3 Larry Villeneuve. Pender underwent hand surgery—one of many the brittle-handed Pender endured—to remove a floating bone from his hand, but he broke his hand in his next fight even though he won a ten-round majority decision over 36-17-2 Ted Olla. Pender started 1955 with a TKO victory over Freddie Mack, a late replacement, and his reward for Paul's successful comeback was 27-0 Gene Fullmer, the future two-time world middleweight champion and Hall of Famer. The result of their Brooklyn fight couldn't have gone any worse for Pender, who broke his left hand in the fourth round and right in the sixth. Pender gutted it out and went the distance, losing a ten-round unanimous decision.

Pender was sidelined for nearly two years when he joined the fire department, returning to the ring in late 1956 to win a ten-round unanimous decision versus Jimmy Skinner. Riding a seven-fight win streak, Pender was matched against popular Ralph Jones (48-2-4), who only two months earlier had defeated Joey Giardello. Pender put on a virtuoso boxing performance to take a convincing ten-round unanimous decision (99-93, 99-94, 98-92) at the Boston Garden. Five months later, Pender captured the New England middleweight title by way of a twelve-round unanimous decision (58-51, 58-50, 59-52). Paul then had a stay-busy fight four months later that he won by ten-round unanimous decision against Gene Hamilton.

In 1960, the reigning world middleweight champion was the great Sugar Ray Robinson, whose National Boxing Association (NBA) version of the world title was vacated because Robinson had not defended his title in more than a year. Pender's home state, Massachusetts, was one of the few states that still recognized Sugar Ray as world champion. Pender's longtime promoter, the inimitable Sam Silverman, convinced Robinson's people to fight a relatively soft touch in Pender. Robinson passed on a $500,000 guaranteed purse to defend his title versus Fullmer to fight Pender for a little more than $80,000 in Boston Garden before more than 10,000 Bostonians rooting for Pender, who as a 6-1 underdog pulled off a major upset, winning a fifteen-round split decision (148-142, 146-142, 138-147) to become world champion.

The rematch was scheduled for April 1960, but Pender injured his heel during training camp and the date was pushed back until June 10, 1960, at Boston Garden. The Pender-Robinson rematch was similar to their original fight despite one hometown score of 149-138, as Pender won another fifteen-round split decision (147-142, 144-146). Pender became the first to defeat Pender twice, and Paul mentioned a unification fight with Fullmer or possibly a light heavyweight challenge to Archie Moore.

A London promoter had been ringside for Pender-Robinson II because of the general belief that Pender would defend against the winner of a British title fight between defending champion Terry Downes and Phil Edwards. Downes (25-6) earned his world title shot by defeating Edwards and future world middleweight champion Giardello. The two threw down on January 14, 1961, at Boston Arena, and Pender turned in one of his finest performances, stopping the London-born Downes in the seventh round. All three judges had Pender leading when he busted up Downes' nose to close the show.

Pender was offered double his purse for his first fight against Downes, $35,000, to fight a rematch in London. Pender has his sights set on the winner of Fullmer vs. Robinson, but the champion changed his mind and accepted an offer to fight Downs in London, later indicating he was considering Carmen Basilio as his next opponent. Pender defended his belt against former world welterweight and middleweight champion Basilio (56-15-7), who had lost his middleweight title bout to Robinson. Pender needed four attempts to make weight, later suffering a five-inch laceration over his left eyelid in the second round. But Paul dropped Basilio for the first time in his long career, sending him into retirement by way of a lopsided fifteen-round unanimous decision (149-135, 147-132, 147-138).

Pender-Downes II was held on July 11, 1961, in Wembley Stadium in London. Pender had a fear of flying and his promoter negotiated a "no plane" clause in the fight contract. He, Silverman, head trainer Al Lacy, and lawyer John Cronin crossed the Atlantic Ocean on the *Queen Elizabeth*. Pender reopened a cut on the bridge of Downes' nose in the second round, both fighters were cut in the third (Downes' cheek, Pender's left eye). Blood was flowing freely, and Lacy, who was like Pender's surrogate father, wouldn't allow Paul to continue fighting with such a serious injury after nine rounds.

Negotiations for Downes-Pender III the following September went back and forth as the respective promoters negotiated purses, television rights, and more. An agreement was finally completed that satisfied both camps, but Downes dislocated his thumb in training camp and surgery was needed. Eventually the fight was made at the Boston Garden on April 7, 1962. No British fighter had ever fought in the United States and returned home with their world title belt. This match was no different in what was an ugly, boring fight. Pender finally got his jab going in the second half of the fight and he went on to barely win back his world title by fifteen-round unanimous decision (145-143, 146-141, 144-143).

A unification title fight against Fullmer was scheduled to be announced for mid-June 1962 in Montana. However, Pender suffered a scalp injury in a car crash and their fight was scrapped when Fullmer agreed to fight Dick Tiger. Rumored fights against European champion Laszlo Papp and future world light heavyweight titlist Jose Torres were not sanctioned.

The thirty-two-year-old Pender had experienced too much of boxing politics for his liking, developing a deep dislike for the sport because of its mob control, and he retired at his peak as world champion.

Pender never received his proper dues, especially for his two victories over Robinson, sending Basilio into retirement. Robinson was in his late thirties when he fought Pender, but he was the world middleweight champion who sported an amazing 144-7-2 pro record.

Paul Pender was a two-time world champion who defeated Hall of Famers Robinson and Basilio. Nobody can ever take those accomplishments away from him.

ALL-NEW ENGLAND

Birth Name:	Paul Pender
Born:	June 20, 1930, in Brookline, Massachusetts
Hometown:	Brookline, Connecticut
Death:	January 12, 2003
Amateurs:	1949 New England champion
Pro Record:	40-6-2 (20 KOs, 3 KOBY)
Pro Titles:	Two-time world middleweight champion (January 22, 1960–July 11, 1961, April 7, 1962–retirement May 7, 1963)
Pro Career:	1949–1962
Height:	5' 10"
Reach:	72"
Stance:	Orthodox
Division:	Middleweight

World Title Fight Record: 5-1 (1 K, 1 KOBY)
Records vs. World Champions: 5-2 (1 KO, 1 KOBY), defeated Ray Robinson* (twice), Carmen Basilio,* Terry Downes (twice); lost to Terry Downes, Gene Fullmer* (* International Boxing HOF)

Manager:	Johnny Buckley
Trainer:	Al Lacy

Notes: Fellow Mass. boxer Al "Red" Priest recommended to Pender that he sign with manager Johnny Buckley; took a position as recreation director at Norfolk Jail and returned to school and completed his degree; later entered politics and worked as a firefighter

No. 11

MARLON STARLING

"Magic Man"
The Underrated Spoiler

Two-time world welterweight champion Marlon "Magic Man" Starling (45-6-1 (27 KOs, 0 KOBY) wasn't an opponent who undefeated fighters wanted to be matched against. The lifelong Hartford (CT) fighter had the unique distinction of defeating four previously undefeated fighters who had a minimum of fifteen pro victories, in addition to never being stopped in fifty-two pro matches.

Starling was groomed as an amateur by coach Johnny Duke; Marlon enjoyed a solid amateur career, highlighted by a silver-medal performance at the 1977 AAU Tournament.

Starling was proud that his fan base was racially balanced during an era of potentially explosive racism.

"There was racism back then, but at Marlon Starling's fights in Hartford, you saw blacks and whites together. I had just as many white fans as blacks, if not more, and most of my friends were white people. I don't know why but I got along with everybody, and everybody got along with me. I first went to the gym when I was 12. My coach, Johnny Duke, was the blackest white dude I knew. I was blessed to be coached by a guy like him. I remember being on a private jet with some corporate people. Johnny was with me, and I bet him $20.00 he couldn't go a minute without saying the word, fuck. He handed me a $20.00 saying, fuck this."

Starling was well aware that it was different, not necessarily better or worse, being a New England fighter.

"The New England states are so small that being called a New England fighter was bigger than being from just one of the six states," Starling insisted. "Ray Leonard once said to me that he could drive through all of New England in six hours. My first fight was in Lowell (MA) at the Silver Mittens when I was 11 ½. And I was scared shit. I liked (Muhammad) Ali, (Cassius) Clay, when I first started boxing. My first robe was like Ali's, black and white, and I wanted to be like him and do what he did in the ring. I lost in the 1971 Silver Mittens quarterfinals, mostly because I was scared. People in the crowd scared me. Ali talked shit, so I started to do the same and I beat another Hartford fighter, Donnie Nelson, who had lost to Olympic gold medalist Ray Seales at the 1972 Olympic Trials."

Starling knocked out Tim LaValley in the third round of his July 27, 1979, pro debut in Hartford, and he rolled to twenty-five straight wins, including a ten-round unanimous decision over 19-2 Floyd Mayweather Sr., and USBA welterweight title winning fight in 1982 with a first-round stoppage of 23-9-1 Kevin Morn.

In 1992, 25-0 Starling put his USBA crown on the line in a twelve-round bout with 14-0 Donald Curry in a battle of undefeated rising welterweight stars in Atlantic City. Curry won the unification fight by spit decision (116-112, 116-112, 113-117) and one and a half years later they squared off for the WBA and IBF world titles in Atlantic City.

Between the two Curry fights, Starling won his next six fights, including his magical run against undefeated opponents, knocking out 16-0 Jose Baret in the fourth round, defeating 21-0 Tommy Ayers by way of a twelve-round majority decision.

Curry was the reigning and defending WBA/IBF World welterweight champion, sporting a perfect 17-0 record, when 31-1 Starling had his first world title shot again in Atlantic City. Starling lost a fifteen-round unanimous decision in their rematch.

Starling returned to the ring two months later, dominating the action for a twelve-round unanimous decision (119-109 x 3) over 23-1-1 Lupe Aquino to regain the USBA welterweight title and add the NABF crown to his display case. Starling lost the NABF title when he dropped a twelve-round majority decision to 17-0-1 Pedro Vilella, but Marlon kept his USBA title with a twelve-round unanimous decision against 28-4-1 Mayweather Sr. in a 1985 rematch, and versus 21-0 Simon Brown via a twelve-round split decision.

An accidental headbutt caused a cut that led to Starling's first loss, excluding the two to Curry, and his USBA crown to 28-1 Johnny Bumphus when the fight was stopped. Bumphus was awarded a win by sixth-round technical decision.

Starling's signature triumph came August 22, 1987, in Colombia, South Carolina, against Olympic gold medalist and defending WBA welterweight world champion Mark Breland (18-0). Starling was behind on the three judges' scorecards (89-99, 92-97, 91-99) going into the eleventh round when Starling knocked out Breland to become world champion. Starling won a decisive twelve-round unanimous decision (118-110, 117-114, 117-112) in his first title defense against 21-4 Fujio Ozaki, coupled with a twelve-round split draw (116-113, 114-114, 114-115) in a rematch with Breland that allowed Starling to retain his title.

"People were surprised I beat (Mark) Breland twice," Starling mentioned. "He was the Olympic champion, but pros are different than amateurs. I remember my first few pro fights. I had big cuts over my eyes from heads, elbows, and shoulders. One opponent said, 'Welcome to the pros.' I wasn't just a fighter; I was a boxer who knew how to fight. I knew what it took to beat Mark Breland. I couldn't believe our second fight was called a draw. You had to knockout Breland to get a decision against him. I was lucky to get out of there."

In his next fight, Starling lost his WBA title belt under a cloud of controversy against 23-0 Tomás Molinares, who unintentionally knocked out Starling right after the bell sounded to signal the conclusion of the sixth round. Molinares was declared the new champion, but that decision was later changed to a "no contest" by the New Jersey Boxing Commission. Starling, who had landed on the canvas for only the second time during his pro career, inexplicably was not renamed WBA welterweight world champion. This confusion led to the implementation of the ten-second warning at the end of each round.

Starling got another world title shot in his next fight (Feb. 4, 1989) against 33-1 defending WBC welterweight world champion Lloyd Honeyghan (33-1) at the famed Caesars Palace in Las Vegas. Starling didn't waste his opportunity, battling Honeyghan throughout the night, dropping him in the ninth and leading going into the eleventh (79-72, 78-85, 78-73), when Marlon scored a technical knockout to become a two-time world welterweight titlist, as well as the lineal champion.

Back home in Hartford, Starling's first WBC title defense was against his overmatched Korean challenger, 27-4-2 Young Kil Jung, who had difficulty winning a round as Starling easily won a twelve-round unanimous decision (119-110, 119-109, 117-112).

In 1990, Starling unsuccessfully moved up in weight, challenging undefeated IBF and lineal world middleweight champion Michael Nunn (34-0) in Las Vegas. Nunn won an oddly scored twelve-round split decision (118-110, 117-111, 114-114). Starling dropped back down to defend his WBC and lineal world welterweight titles that following August in Reno, Nevada, losing a twelve-round majority decision (112-115 x 2, 114-114) to Maurice Blocker (31-1) in what proved to be Starling's final fight.

"I went up two weight classes to fight the best fighter in the world, Michael Nunn (34-0), the reigning IBF Middleweight World Champion," Starling explained. "He didn't win, I lost a majority decision. I wasn't supposed to beat him. That was the first time I had dinner with an opponent after our fight. He did a lot of shit talking leading up to the fight, but that was part of boxing back then for six to eight weeks before the fight. We still talk today."

Marlon Starling was a spoiler, defeating four previously undefeated fighters—Breland, Brown, Ayers, and Baret—underrated and tough as nails, having never being knocked out. All that's missing from his résumé at this writing is a call from the International Boxing Hall of Fame.

During the eighties, Starling was on television more than any fighter in the world other than Ray Leonard.

"My best fight in New England was against Kevin Howard (in 1983 at the Hartford Civic Center)," Starling remembered. "I beat him up because he talked a lot of junk. I won a 12-round decision (60-58, 59-49, 58-51) for the NABF and USBA titles, but it could have been stopped a few times. That was why Ray Leonard chose to him as an opponent for his comeback fight (1984 in Worcester, MA, Leonard won by stopping Howard in the 9th round). I couldn't stand him (Leonard) back then. But, in the end, it was all the publicity he had to do, not him."

Starling looks back at his career wondering why he hasn't been selected for induction in the IBHOF.

"I never ducked nobody," Marlon proudly added. "People didn't want to fight me. I beat Floyd Mayweather Sr. (twice), undefeated Simon Brown, and lost to Maurice Blocker. I stole one when I got a win against Honeyghan. I remember fighting under Madison Square Garden at the Felt Forum. (Mike) Tyson was fighting the next night at Madison Square Garden in the big room. After that, I always fought in Madison Square Garden, not the Felt Forum, and I fought in Atlantic City a lot.

"Boxing used to be good. Today, fighters wait two years to fight a guy. We had to fight the next guy in line. It's always about the money, they don't want prospects to lose. It wasn't the sport I didn't like; it was the people in the sport, but not the fighters. I was robbed by promoters like Bob Arum and Don King, but they beat other fighters more than me."

ALL-NEW ENGLAND

Birth Name:	Marlon Starling
Nickname:	Magic Man
Born:	August 29, 1959, Hartford, Connecticut
Hometown:	Hartford, Connecticut
Amateurs:	97-13, 1975 and 1979 New England Golden Gloves silver medalist, 1977 National AAU Tournament bronze medalist
Pro Record:	45-6-1 (27 KOs, 0 KOBY)
Pro Titles:	WBA world welterweight champion (August 22, 1987–July 29, 1988, WBC world welterweight champion (February 4, 1989–August 19, 1990)
Pro Career:	1979–1990
Height:	5' 8"
Reach:	73"
Stance:	Orthodox
Division:	Welterweight

World Title Fight Record: 4-3-1 (2 KOs, 1 NC)
Records vs. World Champions: 4-5-1 (2 KOs, 1 NC), defeated Lupe Aquino, Simon Brown, Mark Breland; lost to Donald Curry* (twice), Johnny Bumphus, Michael Nunn, Maurice Blocker; draw with Mark Breland; no contest versus Tomas Molinares (* International Boxing HOF)

Trainer: Eddie Futch, Freddie Roach

Notes: Never stopped in fifty-two pro fights; January 1, 1980, in Hartford Civic Center, Starling, in his sixth pro fight, knocked out Charles Newell, who later died due to injuries he suffered during the fight

No. 12

CHAD DAWSON

"Bad"
Beat the Best of the Best

During a six-year stretch from 2006 to 2012, three-time world light heavyweight champion "Bad" Chad Dawson ranked among the top pound for pound fighters in the world, defeating six different world champions in eight fights.

It all started in South Carolina, where Dawson was born before moving to New Haven, Connecticut, in 1988.

Dawson enjoyed being a New England-based fighter despite its unique challenges, noting that eleven of his first twelve pro fights were at the two Connecticut casinos, Foxwoods and Mohegan Sun (his second fight was in Cranston, Rhode Island); his first eighteen were in New England, including Hampton Beach, New Hampshire, and Providence, Rhode Island.

"It was great being a New England fighter," Dawson said, "but it was hard being a New England-based fighter getting recognition. You had to leave to get boxing fans to know your name. But that was the best part, making it out of New England, and becoming world champion. I left New England to train and live in Las Vegas for 4 years. That was the most exciting time of my career. Las Vegas was and still is the destination for fighters."

Dawson started his career as a junior middleweight, knocking out Steve Garrett in the second round at Mohegan Sun Arena. The southpaw mowed down all opponents through his first fourteen pro fights, including 10-1 Willie Lee (KO3) and 31-11 Brett Lally (TKO4); his first title winning performance in 2003, when 14-5-1 Dumont Welliver retired after eight rounds for the vacant WBC Youth World Middleweight Championship.

In his next fight, Dawson didn't lose, but his six-round shutout of Aundalen Sloan was changed to a "no contest" after Chad failed a post-fight drug test in a non-title bout. An impressive ten-round unanimous decision (100-90 x 2, 98-91) win against 8-0-1 Darnell Wilson followed for Dawson in his first WBC Youth title defense at Foxwoods Resort Casino. In 2004, Dawson faced former world champion Carl Daniels (49-4-1) at Foxwoods in his second title defense, stopping Daniels in the seventh round. And Dawson's final WBC Youth title defense came next, at home in New Haven, when 17-4-1 Efrain Garcia was unable to continue after four rounds.

Intra-New England foe Ian Gardner (19-2)—fighting out of Brockton, Massachusetts—and Dawson were matched in 2005 for the vacant North American Boxing Organization (NABO) super middleweight championship in New Haven. Dawson stopped Gardner in the eleventh round, and three fights later, Chad moved up to light heavyweight against fellow Connecticut fighter, defending NABF champion Eric Harding (23-3-1). Dawson overcame a first-round knockdown, cruising to a twelve-round unanimous decision (117-110 x 2, 116-111) to obtain a new title belt.

The Harding fight in 2006 kick-started Dawson's amazing run and also positioned him for his first world title fight on February 3, 2007, in Florida, against defending, undefeated WBC world light heavyweight champion Tomasz Adamek (31-0), an extremely popular Polish fighter. Dawson fully displayed his overall skills throughout the fight, winning a twelve-round unanimous decision and world title.

Dawson successfully defended his WBC strap three times versus, in order, 19-4 Jesus Ruiz (WTKO6), 28-4-1 Epifanio Mendoza (TKO4), and former world champion Glenn Johnson (47-11-1) by twelve-round unanimous decision. Dawson abdicated his WBC title, and in late 1980 he challenged IBF light heavyweight world champion Antonio Tarver (27-4) in Las Vegas. Dawson out-boxed Tarver for a twelve-round unanimous decision (118-109, 117-110 x 2) to become a two-time world champion. In Las Vegas, seven months later, Dawson and Tarver fought again and the second time around played out similarly to their original match as Dawson won another twelve-round unanimous decision (117-111 x 2, 116-112).

A rematch with Johnson (49-12-2) followed in Hartford for Dawson's IBO crown and the Interim WBC World Championship. Dawson, who vacated his IBF title and had been stripped of his WBC crown, defeated Johnson once more by way of a twelve-round unanimous decision (117-111, 115-113 x 2).

"Johnson II was my most memorable fight in New England," Dawson claimed. "The first fight was tough; I won a decision, but it was maybe the toughest fight of my career. A dog fight! The rematch, I beat him easy, winning 10 of 12 rounds."

In only his second fight outside of the United States, 25-0 Dawson traveled to Canada for an August 14, 2010, fight in Montreal against 25-1 Haiti native Jean Pascal, who lived in Montreal, for Dawson's IBO world title and an opportunity for Chad to regain his full WBC world crown. Dawson suffered his first loss as a professional when an accidental headbutt opened a large cut over Dawson's eye, because of which Dawson was unable to continue, as Pascal was awarded a controversial technical knockout victory and the titles. Pascal was winning on the scorecards by scores of 106-103 x 2, 108-101).

Dawson recovered to beat 27-2 Adrian Diaconu nine months later, again in Montreal, by twelve-round unanimous decision (118-110, 117-111, 116-112), setting the stage for a Los Angeles showdown with Philadelphia boxing icon Bernard Hopkins (52-5-2), who had decisioned Pascal to become the WBC light heavyweight world champion. Dawson initially won the WBC and lineal world light heavyweight titles when Hopkins was unable to continue after getting awkwardly thrown from a clinch in round two. Five days later, though, the TKO was ruled a Technical Draw by the WBC, deciding Hopkins was unable to continue because of an injury caused by the referee's mistake, and Hopkins remained the WBC world champion. The California State Athletic Commission followed suit nearly two months later, changing the decision to a "No Contest," and the WBC then ordered a rematch between Dawson and Hopkins.

"The first time I fought Hopkins," Dawson remembered, "he thought I was from Hartford (a lot of people get New Haven and Hartford mixed up)."

Hopkins-Dawson II was held April 28, 2012, in Atlantic City, with Dawson controlling the action and relatively slow pace of the fight, outworking the defending champion for a hard-earned twelve-round majority decision (117-11 x 2, 114-114) to become a three-time world light heavyweight champion.

In a highly unusual act, Dawson decided to drop down one full weight class to challenge Olympic gold medalist and undisputed world super middleweight champion Andre Ward (25-0) for his WBA, WBC, and lineal world titles on September 8, 2012, in Ward's hometown of Oakland, California. A clash of heads in the third round changed what had started out as a chess match, as Ward started to consistently hit Dawson with some telling shots, dropping Dawson to one knee after he caught him with a right to the body and short left hook to the head. Dawson got to his feet for an eight-count, and although buzzed, he managed to survive the round. Dawson was sent to his knee again in the fourth round when Ward struck him with another left hook for another eight-count. A sluggish Dawson was somehow able to avoid Ward's lethal hooks for the next four rounds. Ward finished off Dawson in the tenth round when Dawson ate four punches and voluntarily took a knee. Referee Steve Smoger stepped in, asking Dawson if he wanted to continue, but he didn't receive a response, Dawson looking like a beaten man. Smother called off the fight at that point.

Dawson was still the lineal and WBC light heavyweight world champion, and in mid-2013 he went to Montreal once again, this time to battle dangerous southpaw Adonis Stevenson (20-1), who would be fighting for the first time as a light heavyweight. Fighting in his adopted home as a slight underdog, Stevenson decked Dawson early in the fight with a left hook. Dawson beat the count, but referee Michael Griffin felt Dawson was in a crisis and, questionably, he stopped the fight at 1:11 of the opening round.

A year later, Dawson returned as a cruiserweight to knock out 23-5 George Blade in the first round. Back at light heavyweight, Dawson was upset by 23-4-1 Tommy Karpency via a ten-round split decision (96-94, 94-96, 94-96). Dawson fought only once apiece in 2015, 2016, and 2017, shutting out 12-8 Dion Savage, stopping 23-4 Cornelius White in four, and suffering a tenth round technical knockout loss to world title contender Andrzej Fonfara (28-4).

Dawson didn't fight again until mid-2019, when he won an eight-round unanimous decision over 15-5-2 Quinton Rankin, repeating that exact outcome four months later against 19-8-1 Denis Grachev for the vacant WBC United States light heavyweight title.

"I think I was overlooked because a lot of people didn't think I'd make it as far as I did. I started as a junior middleweight and was still growing. I grew into light heavyweight champion of the world and brought my power with me. I never got the recognition and respect; I had a great career. I was one of the best pound-4-pound fighters for a few years. I take pride in that I fought anybody, anywhere, and in most of those fights I was the underdog, even after I won the world championship. You have to fight the best to be the best. I never turned done the best fighters and I was willing to fight anybody, anywhere, to be a real-world champion."

Chad Dawson may not receive the respect and recognition he richly deserves for beating the best of the best—Hopkins, Tarver, Johnson, and Adamek—but he was at the top of mountain for his incredible six-year span.

ALL-NEW ENGLAND

Birth Name:	Chad Dawson
Nickname:	Bad
Born:	July 13, 1982, in Hartsville, South Carolina
Hometown:	New Haven, Connecticut
Amateurs:	67-13, 2000 US National Under-19 Champion and World Junior Championships bronze medalist
Pro Record:	36-5 (19 KOs, 3 KOBY)
Pro Titles:	Three-time world light heavyweight champion: WBC February 3, 2007–July 11, 2008 and April 29, 2012–June 8, 2013; IBF (October 11, 2008–May 27, 2009)
Pro Career:	2001–2019
Height:	6' 1"
Reach:	76.5"
Stance:	Southpaw
Division:	Cruiserweight, light heavyweight, super middleweight, middleweight, and junior middleweight

World Title Fight Record: 8-3, 1 NC (3 KOs, 2 KOBY)
Records vs. World Champions: 8-3, 2 NC (1 KO, 2 KOBY), defeated Carl Daniels, Tomasz Adamek, Glen Johnson (twice), Antonio Tarver (twice), Adrian Diaconu, Bernard Hopkins*; lost to Jean Pascal, Andre Ward, Adonis Stevenson (* International Boxing HOF)

Manager:	Al Haymon
Trainer:	Dan Birmingham, Floyd Mayweather Sr., Emanuel Steward, John Scully, Eddie Mustafa Muhammad

Notes: His father, Rick, was a boxer; in 2019, Dawson opened Champion Gym in New Haven

No. 13

KID KAPLAN

Momma Didn't Want Her Son to Box

Long before Ukrainian world champions such as the Klitschko brothers Wladimir and Vitali, Vasyl Lomachenko, and Oleksandr Usyk, Kid Kaplan was the preeminent boxer from Ukraine. At the age of five, he emigrated to the United States, where he settled in Meriden, Connecticut.

Kaplan (107-12-13, 27 KOs) went on to have a great fifteen-year pro boxing career, fighting the elite of his era, defeating future Hall of Fame boxers like fellow Nutmeg State fighter Battling Battalino, in addition to Jackie Fields and Sammy Mandell.

He sold fruit for five cents a day and learned to box as a teenager, though it was in secrecy because his mother didn't want him to box. In fact, the first few fights he had were under the assumed name Benny Miller until his father approved and convinced his wife that their son should fight.

His first pro fight was in 1918, and the beloved Jewish boxer went on to have more than fifty fights in the first four years of his pro career. By late 1922, he started fighting world-class opponents such as 38-13-8 Babe Herman, who handed Kaplan a loss in twelve rounds on points in the first of their seven fights (Kaplan won two and the had four draws) through 1923.

Kaplan's first major win was against future world champion Jimmy Goodrich (73-17-13), in 1923 at Madison Square Garden on points in a ten-round match. Kaplan took full advantage of a tournament to determine the world featherweight champion after title-holder Johnny Dundee had retired. Kaplan went through 18-8-4 Angel Diaz (KO3), 38-12-6 Bobby Garcia (KO4), and 25-3 Jose Lombardo (KO4) to qualify for the world title fight on January 2, 1925, at MSG against 100-16-20 Danny Kramer. Kaplan knocked out Kramer in the ninth round to become world champion.

In 1925, Kaplan defended his world title twice against his archrival 72-21-19 Herman, fighting a draw in Waterbury (CT) and then notching a fifteen-round unanimous decision win in MSG. Hurley Stadium in Hartford was built to host the World Featherweight Championship bout between defending champion Kaplan and challenger Garcia (53-25-7). Kaplan stopped Garcia in the tenth round of their rematch, and a week later relinquished his world title because he was unable to make weight (126 lbs.) as a featherweight anymore.

Two years later, Kaplan won a ten-round bout on points at the Polo Grounds in New York City against 24-1-1 Fields, the 1924 Olympic gold medalist and future two-time world welterweight champion. In 1927, Kaplan was stopped in the eighth round by future Hall of Famer Jimmy McLaren, who later admitted Kaplan hit harder than any opponent he faced, revealing that Kaplan broke his jaw during this fight.

Kaplan defeated future two-time world champion Johnny Jadick in 1929, when Jadick was disqualified in the seventh round for persistent holding. In 1930, Kaplan defeated a pair of future world champions, 69-21-4 Maurice Holtzer and 27-6-2 Battalino, both by points in ten-round fights. The following year, Kaplan decisioned Mandell, and after losing on points to Cocoa Kid (27-5-2), Kaplan retired.

Known for his incredible stamina and fan-friendly style, Kid Kaplan was a Ukrainian gift to boxing, and New Englanders benefited from his relocation to Connecticut, where he was known as "The Meridian Buzz Saw."

ALL-NEW ENGLAND

Birth Name: Louis Kaplan
Nickname: Kid
Born: October 15, 1901, in Kiev, Ukraine
Hometown: Meriden, Connecticut
Pro Record: 107-23-13 (27 KOs, 3 KOBY)
Pro Titles: World featherweight champion (December 18, 1925–July 6, 1926)
Pro Career: 1918–1933
Height: 5' 2"
Reach: 62.5"
Stance: Orthodox
Division: Featherweight

World Title Fight Record: 3-0-1 (3 KOs)
Records vs. World Champions: 6-1 (0 KOs, 1 KOBY), Battling Battalino,* Maurice Holtzer, Johnny Jadick, Jimmy Goodrich, Sammy Mandell,* Jackie Fields*; lost to Jimmy McLarnin* (* International Boxing HOF)

Manager: Denny McMahon, Billy Gibson
Trainer: Whitey Bimstein

Notes: International Boxing Hall of Fame, Class of 2003; known as a gentleman who never cursed in public; inducted into the International Jewish Sports Hall of Fame

No. 14

LOU BRUILLARD

Switch Hitting Success

Canadian import Lou Brouillard fought the best of the best during the 1930s, capturing world middleweight and welterweight titles. He also defeated six Hall of Famers, culminating with his induction into the International Boxing Hall of Fame.

Unusual, to say the least, is that Brouillard started his career as a right-hander, only to covert to the southpaw stance because he broke a few ribs on his right side, which prohibited him from unloading with his right hand.

Born in Saint-Eugene, Quebec, Canada, Brouillard (100-31-2, 37 KOs) resettled in Worcester, Massachusetts, turning pro in 1928 with a first-round knockout of Billy Krake in Willimantic, Connecticut. Brouillard won sixty-one of his first sixty-eight pro fights, primarily against New England fighters, before he got his first world title shot on October 23, 1931, at the Boston Garden.

In the first title fight in Massachusetts in eleven years after boxing was legalized in the Commonwealth, Brouillard won a fifteen-round unanimous decision over 76-28-12 Young Jack Thompson to become the NBA welterweight world champion. Four fights and three months later, Brouillard lost his title belt by way of a ten-round unanimous decision in Chicago to 64-6-2 Jackie Fields.

In the Boston Garden on May 15, 1931, Brouillard stopped New England rival Al Mello (43-9) in the eighth round for a rare double, both the New England middleweight and welterweight titles.

Brouillard, who was still the New England welterweight champion, registered a statement victory in 1932, taking a ten-round split decision from 49-7-3 Jimmy McLarin. The first plateau of Brouillard's pro career was in 1933–34, when he was 10-3, including triumphs over 120-18-3 Mickey Walker (PTS10) at the Boston Garden, 48-8-4 Ben Jeby (KO7) at the Polo Grounds in New York City for the NYSAC World middleweight crown, and a pair against 42-11-3 Bob Olin (DEC10 and PTS10).

Brouillard continued to fight the best of the best in 1935–36, defeating 108-9-20 Young Corbett II (PTS10) in San Francisco and 71-4-9 Gustave Roth (SDEC15) in Paris, but three losses to 106-20-10 Marcel Thil (DEC12, DQ4 and 6), suffering defeats against 90-19-17 Al McCoy (DEC10), 18-1 Fred Apostoli (PTS10), and 88-4-2 Teddy Yarosz (PTS10).

His three fights with Thil were held in his opponent's backyard in Paris. His first Thil fight was so competitive, Lou was given a rematch offer for two months later, only this time it was for Thil's newly gained International Boxing Union (IBU) Middleweight World Championship. Brouillard, though, was disqualified in their second and third encounters for landing blows below the belt.

In retrospect, Brouillard should have probably retired after the Thil trilogy, losing ten of his final twenty-seven pro fights, although he continued to face a few world-class opponents such as Yarosz, 37-3-5 Gus Lesnevich (LPTS10), and 20-4-1 Lloyd Marshall (LDEC10).

Lou Brouillard, named Canada's fourth greatest boxer ever, may never have won one hundred career fights if he hadn't switched from righty to lefty.

ALL-NEW ENGLAND

Birth Name: Lucian Pierre Brouillard
Born: May 23, 1911, in Saint Eugene, Quebec, Canada
Hometown: Worcester, Massachusetts
Death: September 14, 1984
Pro Record: 100-31-2 (57 KOs, 1 KOBY)
Pro Titles: World welterweight (October 13, 1931–January 28, 1932) and world middleweight (August 9, 1933–October 30, 1933)
Pro Career: 1928–40
Height: 5' 7"
Reach: 72"
Stance: Southpaw
Division: Middleweight and welterweight

World Title Fight Record: 2-2 (1 KO, 0 KOBY)
Records vs. World Champions: 8-9 (1 KO, 0 KOBY), defeated Young Jack Thomson (2), Jimmy McLarin,* Mickey Walker,* Ben Jeby, Bob Olin (2), Young Corbet III*; lost to Marcel Thil (3),* Jackie Fields,* Vince Dundee, Fred Apostoli,* Teddy Yarosz,* Gus Lesnevich, Anton Christoforidis (* International Boxing HOF)

Manager: Maurice Lemoine, Johnny Buckley

Notes: International Boxing Hall of Fame, Class of 1990; started boxing as a righthander, switched to southpaw due to a broken rib on right side that hampered his ability to hit with his right hand; stopped only one time (Tiger Jack Fox) in 133 pro fights

No. 15

JOHN RUIZ

"The Quietman"
First Latino World Heavyweight Champion

"Follow Your Dream" was John Ruiz's mantra, and the Puerto Rican-American certainly followed this, right up to capturing a world heavyweight title not once, but twice as the first world heavyweight champion of Latino heritage.

Born in Methuen, Massachusetts, he soon moved with his mother to Puerto Rico, where he lived until he moved at the age of seven to live in a housing project in Chelsea, Massachusetts.

"It was a long road from growing up in the Boston area (Chelsea)," Ruiz explained. "I live in Florida now and lived 12 years in Las Vegas. I do miss the four seasons and all the family and friends I left behind. Training in the snow and cold does build character. I first moved because I wanted to clear my mind. It was nice going somewhere else. I got stuck in a routine living at home and moving to Las Vegas helped me focus on the fights.

"I left New England to train in Florida, Las Vegas, and the Poconos. I liked living in Las Vegas a lot. I was looking to move where there wasn't a state tax. It was a great place for me to go because most of the big boxing was and still is in Las Vegas. I loved it there, training day and night, without any problems. We always brought in sparring partners wherever I had training camp, but a lot of them wanted to go to Las Vegas. I mostly kept to myself (at training camp). I never did too many other things. I would train and then go right back to my room. No goofing around. I do have some great memories of this sport, like fighting at a dog track (Wonderland Greyhound Park in Revere, MA), and so many other nice spots all over New England."

After enjoying a decorated amateur career as a light heavyweight, it ended disappointedly because he lost at home to Jeremy Williams at the 1992 US Olympic Trials in Worcester, Massachusetts.

"I had a good time as an amateur," Ruiz noted. "I remember training in Colorado Springs and traveling to Italy. I was more relaxed with the amateur style; the pros was just business. We had some big names on the USA Boxing Team. There was Chris Byrd, Raul Marquez, Oscar de la Hoya, Larry Donald, and others. I remember talking with Larry Donald, who beat me in the finals of the National Golden Gloves in Iowa, when a kid came by on a bike and grabbed his baseball cap, right off his head. Funny thing was he took off chasing him and got his cap back."

Ruiz made a conscious effort to be a heavyweight, realizing there was much more money available to heavyweights than light heavyweights, hiring strength and conditioning coach Keith McGrath. John only weighed 184 pounds for his August 20, 1992, pro debut in Atlantic City, taking a four-round unanimous decision from Kevin Parker. "The Quiet Man" gradually built his body up through his first seventeen pro fights into a solid heavyweight. In his fifteenth pro fight though, he ran into 14-0-1 Sergey Kobozev and lost by way of a ten-round split decision. But he bounced back to win his next four bouts, and then lost a questionable twelve-round split decision (115-113, 113-115, 110-118) to 15-1 Danell Nicholson for the International Boxing Organization (IBO) at Foxwoods Resort Casino for the vacant International Boxing Organization (IBO) World heavyweight title.

Once again Ruiz responded in positive fashion, winning seven in a row, including an impressive ten-round unanimous decision over 23-0 Boris Powell (98-92 x 2, 97-93), then stopping 15-4 Derrick Roddy via a second-round knockout for the WBC international heavyweight crown. Ruiz positioned himself as the favorite in the *Young Heavyweights*

Tournament airing live on HBO, but he drew hard-hitting Samoan David Tua (22-0) in the series opener. Warned about Tua's powerful punching ability, the two fighters raced across the ring, and Tua connected with a devastating left hook that seriously hurt Ruiz, who never saw it coming, followed by a half dozen shots, punctuated by a vicious right that knocked out Ruiz only nineteen seconds into their high-profile fight. To his credit, on the ride home he demanded that as soon as he was off suspension he wanted to get back in the ring.

"There was no quitting in me," Ruiz spoke about fighting after his loss to Tua. "I had no choice. I had a family to support, and I fought for them as much as myself. I learned never to have a feeling-out first round. It's a fight from the first round on. It did get me more focused. You can't make errors, or you'll end up on the canvas."

Three months later, Ruiz stopped journeyman Doug Davis in the sixth round and started yet another comeback, showing his determination and perseverance, and he climbed the ratings ladder into contention. In 1998, he won a twelve-round split decision over 56-6 Jimmy Thunder for the vacant NABF heavyweight title, followed by his first NABF title defense against former world heavyweight champion Tony Tucker (56-6), who Ruiz stopped in the eleventh round by technical knockout, registered a fourth-round stoppage of 19-1-1 Jerry Ballard, repeating that result against 16-1 Fernely Feliz, and then blasting out 25-6 Thomas Williams in two.

Ruiz's former stablemate Lennox Lewis didn't want to face his mandatory challenger Ruiz, but Team Ruiz sued the WBA, claiming its rules entitled him to its world title fight. Ruiz won his appeal, but undisputed champion Lewis forfeited his WBA world title belt rather than defend against Ruiz by fighting Michael Grant. Ruiz was matched against living legend Evander Holyfield (36-4-1) for the vacant crown in Las Vegas. Holyfield became the first to capture the world heavyweight title four times; however, the twelve-round unanimous decision (116-112, 114-113, 114-113) was so controversial that many reporters and fans felt Ruiz deserved the decision. Team Ruiz quickly petitioned the WBA for an immediate rematch, which was granted for March 3, 2001, at Mandalay Bay Resort and Casino in Las Vegas.

That specific date forever changed Ruiz's life, as well as that of members of his team, family, and close friends. He had gained a lifetime of invaluable experience in terms of "dirty" fighting in Holyfield-Ruiz I, using it to his advantage in their rematch. Holyfield, who was known as one of the most effective "dirty fighters" in boxing history, had broken Ruiz's orbit bone with a well-placed elbow in their original fight, and he often went south with punches as well.

Ruiz, though, was ready this time. He joined Riddick Bowe as the only fighter to floor Holyfield, vengefully responding from getting hit below the belt with a low blow of his own, and emerged at the end with a twelve-round unanimous decision (116-110, 115-111, 114-111) to become the first Latino world heavyweight champion (Mexican-American Andy Ruiz, no relation, became the second Latino world heavyweight champion in 2019 when he knocked out Anthony Joshua).

As heavyweight champion of the world (still one of the most coveted individual titles in sports), celebrity status soon followed for Ruiz. Thousands lined the streets for a celebratory parade and even more filled a stadium in Puerto Rico to celebrate his accomplishment, honored back home in Chelsea, and he met President George W. Bush in the White House (see picture below).

Ruiz and Holyfield completed their trilogy with an ugly draw; 32-0-1 Kirk Johnson was disqualified in the tenth round for his repeated low blows; and then Ruiz fought another legend, 47-1 Roy Jones Jr., on March 1, 2003, at the Thomas & Mack Center in Las Vegas. Ruiz never should have taken this fight, largely due to personal issues at that time, but their PPV event marked the largest payday of his career. Despite weighing thirty-three pounds more than Jones, Ruiz was unable to use his size advantage, claiming referee Jay Nady wouldn't allow him to fight aggressively, and Jones took a twelve-round unanimous decision to join Bob Fitzsimmons as the only middleweight world champion to also become world heavyweight titlist.

Nine months later, Ruiz fought 35-4-1 Hasim Rahman in a battle of former world heavyweight champions in Atlantic City for the Interim WBA heavyweight championship. Ruiz won a twelve-round unanimous decision (118-110, 116-112, 115-114), and Jones was declared WBA

Champion in Recess because of delays to defend his title against no. 1 contender Vitali Klitschko, who made it clear that he didn't want to fight no. 2 challenger Rahman for the Interim moniker. No. 3 Tua turned down the opportunity to fight Rahman as well, but no. 5 Ruiz quickly accepted. In February of the following year, when Jones announced that he was returning to fight in the light heavyweight division, Ruiz officially became the two-time WBA world heavyweight champion when he was elevated to that position.

In the first world heavyweight fight contested between Latinos, Ruiz successfully defended his belt against 24-2 Fres Oquendo in Madison Square Garden. Ruiz retained his WBA title with an eleventh round stoppage. And seven months later, at the same venue, Ruiz overcame two knockdowns and a one-point penalty administrated by referee Randy Neumann for a dramatic comeback victory against 38-4-1 Andrew Golota, winning a twelve-round unanimous decision (113-112, 114-111, 114-111).

The following April, again at MSG, Ruiz lost his title to James Toney by way of a twelve-round unanimous decision (116-111 twice, 115-112), and after the fight he emotionally and prematurely announced his retirement. He soon came out of retirement prior to the announcement that Toney had tested positive for a steroid, which resulted in the outcome being changed to a "no contest," and Ruiz was reinstated as WBA world champion.

Ruiz traveled to Germany that following December to fight seven foot, 324-pound Russian challenger Nikolai Valuev (42-0), who won a controversial twelve-round majority decision (116-113, 116-112, 114-114) in which the majority of 10,000 fans booed because they felt the decision was unfair.

Up next for Ruiz was another trip to Germany to fight a different Russian, 21-0-1 prospect Ruslan Chagaev, who won a twelve-round split decision (117-111, 116-112, 114-115). Ruiz managed to get two more WBA world title fights, losing another twelve-round decision in Germany to 48-1 Valuev (who had lost his title belt to Chagaev) for the vacant WBA strap. In 2010, Ruiz went to Manchester, England, for his final world title shot against 23-1 David Haye, who had beaten Valuev for the title. Hayes dropped Ruiz four times, including twice in the opening round, en route to his successful title defense by ninth-round technical knockout when Ruiz's corner threw in the towel. Ruiz soon announced his retirement after eighteen years as a prizefighter.

"I'm super proud to be the first Latino heavyweight champion of the world," Ruiz emphasized. "Latinos had won world titles in all the other divisions, but never a heavyweight, and it was a great experience for me and my team. It was humbling to reach that part of my career and be on top of the world. I can't put into words how I feel. I still get chills thinking about it."

No boxer ever got more out of their God-given skills than John Ruiz.

ALL-NEW ENGLAND

Birth Name:	John Ruiz
Nickname:	The Quietman
Born:	January 4, 1972, in Methuen, Massachusetts
Hometown:	Chelsea, Massachusetts
Amateurs:	50-5, New England, USA Boxing National and Los Angeles Olympic Festival champion, defeated Torsten May, the 1992 Olympic gold medal winner from Germany, at a dual meet
Pro Record:	44-9-1 (30 KOs, 2 KOBY)
Pro Career:	1992–2010
Height:	6' 2"
Reach:	78"
Stance:	Orthodox
Division:	Heavyweight

World Title Fight Record: 5-6-1 (1 KO, 1 KOBY)
Records vs. World Champions: 3-6-1 (1 KO, 1 KOBY), defeated Tony Tucker, Evander Holyfield,* Hasim Rahman; lost to David Haye, Nikolay Valuev (twice), Ruslan Chagaev, Roy Jones, Jr., Evander Holyfield*; draw with Evander Holyfield,* No Contest with James Toney (* International Boxing HOF)

Manager/Advisor:	Norman Stone, Anthony Cardinale
Trainer:	Gabe LaMarca, Norman Stone, Manny Siaca Sr., Miguel Diaz

Notes: Criticized for his jab-and-clinch style that led to ugly fights; an all-star football player at Chelsea High; Oscar de la Hoya accidently gave Ruiz his nickname at a USA boxing tournament in Lake Placid, New York, when somebody asked Oscar if he knew where Ruiz was, he referred to John as "the quiet guy," which eventually turned into the grammatically incorrect "The Quietman"

No. 16

GEORGE DIXON

"Little Chocolate"
Good Things Come in Small Packages

Standing only five foot three and a half inches and weighing merely eighty-seven pounds when he started his boxing career (leading to his "Little Chocolate" nickname), George Dixon was a record-setting pioneer as the first black to capture a world title in any sport, and also the first two-time and three-time world featherweight champion. Recognized for developing "shadowboxing" back in the nineteenth century, George was a charter inductee in the International Boxing Hall of Fame.

A four-time, two-division world champion, Dixon was born in Nova Scotia, Canada, moving to Boston around 1900, and he reportedly fought in as many as 800 fights because of his hundreds of unrecorded exhibitions in vaudeville venues. His official pro debut was November 1, 1886, when he knocked out Young Johnson in the third round of their fight in Halifax.

Dixon claimed the World Bantamweight Championship in 1888 after a bout with Tommy "Spider" Kelly, but he wasn't officially crowned until two years later, after he stopped Nunc Wallace in the eighteenth round of their title fight in England. He lost a close decision July 1, 1898, to British lightweight champion Ben Jordan at New York's Leno Club on points in twenty-five rounds.

77

Targeting Solly Smith to complete their trilogy, Dixon changed gears when Smith lost his world title to Dave Sullivan after suffering a broken arm in the fifth round, and Dixon regained the world featherweight title when Sullivan was disqualified in the tenth round after holding the belt for merely forty-five days.

Dixon eventually went on a whirlwind tour, fighting all across the US as often as three times a month in Boston, Providence, New York City, Philadelphia, Baltimore, Louisville, Pittsburgh, and other cities. Most of his early title fights were against nondescript challengers, some of whom had few, and even in one case zero, pro fights. His level of opposition increased in 1895 when he was matched against Young Griffo, Franke Erne, Torpedo Billy Murphy, Pedlar Palmer, and Solly Smith. In 1900, he faced Terry McGovern twice, and Abe Attell thrice in 1901, and he returned to England for a long series of matches through 1905, facing Palmer and Jim Driscoll, among the notables, prior to returning to the States to close out his career in 1906.

Dixon's life, sadly, went downhill rapidly after he stopped boxing. He was living and begging on the streets of New York City, friendless other than (according to Dixon) John L. Sullivan. On his own because he had fallen into poor health, he died in the alcohol ward of Bellevue Hospital at the age of thirty-seven.

George Dixon was ahead of his time, remembered by many as a pioneer who left his mark on boxing that still remains to this day.

ALL-NEW ENGLAND

Birth Name:	George Dixon
Nickname:	Little Chocolate
Born:	July 29, 1870, in Halifax, Nova Scotia, Canada
Hometown:	Boston, Massachusetts
Death:	January 6, 1908
Pro Record:	68-30-57 (36 KOs, 6 KOBY)
Pro Titles:	World bantamweight champion (1890–vacated 1891), three-time world featherweight champion (1891–1896, 1897–1897, 1898–1900)
Pro Career:	1886–1906
Height:	5' 3.5"
Reach:	66"
Stance:	Orthodox
Division:	Featherweight and bantamweight

World Title Fight Record: 21-3-3 (12 KOs, 1 KOBY)

Records vs. World Champions: 2-10-7 (1 KO, 2 KOBY), defeated Solly Smith, Pedlar Palmer; lost to Young Corbett II,* Pedlar Palmer (twice), Danny Dougherty,* Abe Attell,* Frank Erne* (twice), Terry McGovern* (twice), Solly Smith; draw with Abe Attell (twice), Pedlar Palmer, Frank Erne,* Young Griffo* (thrice) (* International Boxing HOF); as world featherweight champion he established a vaudeville troupe, "George Dixon Specialty Co.," which toured throughout North America

Manager:	Tim O'Rourke

Notes: International Boxing Hall of Fame, Class of 1990; may have had as many as 800 unrecorded exhibitions in vaudeville halls; first black champion in any sport, first world featherweight champion, first Canadian-born boxing champion, first boxing champion to regain the belt after a defeat; inducted into Canada's Sports Hall of Fame and ranked sixth in Nova Scotia's greatest athletes in history; in 2021, was designated as National Historic Person

No. 17

JOE WALCOTT

"Barbados Demon"
The Original Joe Walcott

Often mistaken for the Hall of Fame heavyweight fighter with the same name, "Jersey" Joe Walcott, who took his idol's nickname "Barbados Demon," Joe Walcott was one of the most famous boxers of his era, along with other black Boston fighters in the late 1890s and early twentieth century such as Sam Langford, George Dixon, and George Godfrey.

Born in Guyana, Walcott spent much of his childhood in Barbados until at the age of fourteen he wanted to see the world, becoming a cabin attendant on a ship sailing to his future hometown, Boston. There he worked as a porter, piano mover, and did odds job until he took a steady job in a gym. There he became popular as a capable opponent for even the best boxers until he turned pro in 1892.

Fighting primarily in Boston and New York City during his early years as a professional, Walcott (87-24-24, 57 KOs) increased the level of his opposition in 1895 when he fought a draw with Mysterious Billy Smith, who Joe ended up fighting five more times. He lost for only the second time in his forty-second fight, fifteen rounds on points to George "Kid" Lavigne. Two and a half years later, in Walcott's first world title fight, Lavigne knocked him out in the twelfth round in San Francisco.

Walcott's second world title fight shot didn't go any better for him, losing in twenty rounds on points to 28-12-16 Smith for the World Welterweight Championship. In 1990, Walcott fought light heavyweight Joe Choynski, who had a sixteen-pound and a full foot height advantage. A 3-1 underdog when the fight started, Walcott dropped Choynski five times in the opening round, and referee Johnny White stopped the fight in the seventh round fearing for Choynski's life.

Finally, in 1901, Walcott became the world welterweight champion, stopping 34-7-5 Ruibe Ferns in the fifth round—the result of Walcott's ferocious attack, which led to his catchy nickname "Barbados Demon."

Controversy surrounded Walcott's first world title defense, however, when last-minute replacement referee Duck Sullivan shockingly stopped the fight against Dixie Kid in the twentieth round in a fight Walcott had dominated, disqualifying Walcott for no clear reason. This fight was disregarded as a title fight and Walcott continued as champion after it was later revealed that the referee had bet on Dixie Kid.

Walcott and Langford squared off for Walcott's crown in 1904 at Lake Massabesic Coliseum in Manchester, New Hampshire. Two of the most gifted boxers in the world fought to a fifteen-round draw. Langford controlled the first half of the bout, dropping Walcott to one knee in the third, but Walcott came on strong in the second half, closing hard to earn a draw and retain his world title belt. Two fights later, Walcott faced world lightweight champion Joe Gans (144-9-18) in a non-title fight in San Francisco. Gans was in charge the first ten rounds, displaying his advanced defensive skills while banging Walcott's body to set up head shots. Walcott finished strong once again in what had turned into an entertaining back-and-forth encounter. Walcott and Gans fought to a twenty-round draw, and it was later discovered that the gritty Walcott had suffered a broken elbow on his right arm in the fourth round.

Chelsea, Massachusetts, was the scene in 1906 for two successive world title fights against 33-7-10 Honey Mellody from nearby Charlestown (a Boston district), who won the first match up in fifteen rounds on points. And one month later, as the new world champion,

Walcott quit in the 132nd round, claiming his left arm had been injured in the ninth round.

The Mellody fights were the last hurrah for Walcott, who continued fighting five more years but he was a shell of himself after being involved in so many ring wars. Having blown a small fortune, relatively speaking, that he had earned during his boxing career, Walcott ended up a custodian at Madison Square Garden.

"Barbados Demon" Joe Walcott will be remembered as a three-time world champion and the OJW (original).

ALL-NEW ENGLAND

Birth Name: Joe Walcott
Nickname: Barbados Demon
Born: March 13, 1873, in Demerara, Guyana
Hometown: Boston, Massachusetts
Death: October 4, 1935
Amateurs: 1938–39 Connecticut state champion
Pro Record: 87-24-24 (57 KOs, 9 KOBYs)
Pro Titles: Three-time world welterweight champion (July 3, 1903–April 29, 1904; July 10, 1906; October 16, 1906; December 18, 1901–June 23, 1912)
Pro Career: 1892–1911
Height: 5' 1.5"
Reach: 65"
Stance: Orthodox
Division: Welterweight and lightweight

World Title Fight Record: 4-4-3 (2 KOs, 2 KOBY)
Records vs. World Champions: 4-7-6 (1 KO, 1 KOBY), defeated Mysterious Billy Smith (twice), George Gardner, James Ferns; lost to Dixie Kid,* Philadelphia Jack O'Brien,* George Gardner, Mysterious Billy Smith (twice), Kid Lavigne (twice); draw with Joe Gans,* Sam Langford,* Philadelphia Jack O'Brien,* Mysterious Billy Smith (twice) (* International Boxing HOF)

Manager: Tom O'Rourke

Notes: International Boxing Hall of Fame, Class of 1991; his nickname came from his ferocity in the ring and willingness to fight anybody; he accidentally shot and killed Nelson Hall in 1904, bullets from the automatic weapon cost Walcott several fingers and kept him sidelined for a year and a half

No. 18

DEMETRIUS ANDRADE

"Boo Boo"
Boxing's Boogeyman of the Twenty-First Century

Before he hangs up his gloves, three-time, two-division world champion Demetrious Andrade could certainly crack New England's all-time top ten, if not higher, based on his rich amateur pedigree, sterling professional record, and tremendous overall boxing accomplishments. He is the only active fighter on the *New England's Greatest Boxer*'s top twenty-five list.

Through the middle of 2020, Andrade sported a perfect 31-0 (19 KOs) pro record at the age of thirty-one, but the knock against him was the lack of a statement victory against a celebrated rival. But it wasn't his fault. He can only fight the opponent across the ring from him. The three superstars during Andrade's career—Saul "Canelo" Alvarez, Floyd Mayweather Jr., and Gennady Golovkin—refused to fight him because of the old risk and reward reasoning. Andrade's superior skills would have been dangerous for them because he is a consummate boxer with pop who is difficult to fight. Styles make fights, and Alvarez, Mayweather, and Golovkin realized that if the outcome of their fight came down to hitting without being hit, Andrade would have had the advantage.

"It's good to be recognized in the boxing world by fans," Andrade offered. "Anybody can win a 50-50 fight. 'Canelo' says he we won't fight me because I haven't fought anybody. If that's the way he thinks, why wouldn't he fight me? They use that and the payday excuse. 'Canelo' makes the most money. He is the most popular but there are better fighters than him. 'Canelo,' 'GGG' (Gennadiy Golovkin), the Charlo brothers (Jermell and Jarmell), Billy Joe (Saunders) . . . none of them will fight me. 'GGG' held his title hostage and prevented others from unifying. I'd fight either of the Charlos. Billy Joe was supposed to fight me, but he got caught using steroids. I guess he needed the money. I can only control what I can control. I can't be frustrated just because things haven't worked out. Fans pay $75 to watch guys to see knockouts, so 'Canelo' fought (Amir) Khan but not Demetrious Andrade."

Andrade, who is nicknamed "Boo Boo," hasn't lost a fight since 2008, when he was robbed in the quarterfinals of the Olympics in favor of South Korean Kim Jung-joo (11–9) in Beijing, China. In some ways it would be a prelude to what would happen to him in the pro ranks, too often frustrating stretches due to promotional problems and lucrative fights falling through, plus misguided and unfair criticism of him picking and choosing his opponents. Bottom line, Andrade was arguably the most avoided fighter in the world throughout his professional career, which consistently stalled off and on, costing him millions of dollars.

Andrade was born with a special gift, which was illuminated during one of the most decorated amateur careers in USA history, highlighted by his gold medal performance at the 2007 World Amateur Boxing Championships in Chicago. He started boxing at the tender age of six when his father and head trainer Paul Andrade first brought him to the gym when his older brother, Michael, was training. Demetrius went on to win the 2005 and 2006 US National Championships and 2006 and 2007 National Golden Gloves Championships.

At the prestigious Pan-American Games in Brazil, he defeated three well known boxers—John Jackson, Carlos Prada, and Diego Gabriel Chaves—leading up to the championship final, where he was ripped off by a hometown boxer, Brazilian Pedro Lima, by an obviously questionable score, 7-6.

To qualify as the USA Olympic Boxing Team in the welterweight division, he had to defeat future professional world champion Keith Thurman twice, 27-13 at the US Olympic Trials, 18-14 at the USA Olympic Box-Offs.

"I had fun starting out at 5 and I had my first fight at 6," Andrade said. "My dad had his gym, and I was also able to travel to gyms in New England. As a young fighter, it was exciting to watch fighters in the gym working out like Vinny Paz, Micky Ward, Peter Manfredo Jr., and Chad Dawson. They were exciting to see, and that boxing was exciting for me. I hoped to go on the same path as them; I looked up to those guys. They set the bar for me back then. I also enjoyed talking to old-time trainers like (Bobby) 'Tiny' Ricci. He always kept my spirits up in the gym.

"The most critical part of my life was in the amateurs. I learned from traveling around the world to tournaments. It was my schooling, not only in the ring, but I learned how to negotiate. It was a great experience; nothing like it. We were all representing our country, but we used to talk about fighters from our area being the best in the United States. We may have all been on an all-star team, but I still represented New England.

"Everything was a lesson for me—win, lose or draw. Whatever happened helped me in many ways, even getting robbed at the Olympics. I was on my path of learning. The (Olympic scoring) system sucks but, hey, you get screwed in life. I prefer making money. There was no money in the amateurs, unless you had sponsorships, but it was cool. I did my years (in the amateurs) to get where I am today, and my career isn't completed yet. The boxing business is tough, but life isn't easy, and you just need to do your best."

Disappointed yet proud to represent his country at the Olympics, Andrade turned pro on October 23, 2008, in Washington, knocking out Patrick Cape in the second round. His copromoters, Banner Promotions and Star Boxing, slowly developed Andrade and it was difficult to find opponents for him because of his reputation from the amateurs and impressive start to his pro career. He stepped up in 2011 during a three-fight streak against 28-12 Grady Brewer (DEC10)—well known because of his experience in *The Contenders* reality television show—28-18-2 Saul Duran (RTD3), and 30-10 Angel Hernandez (20-10). In 2013, he won a lopsided ten-round decision over 30-3 Freddie Hernandez, positioning him for his first world title fight.

Andrade was slated to challenge defending WBO champion Zaurbek Baysangurov on July 7, 2007, in Kyiv, Ukraine, who eventually was stripped of his title belt after suffering a back injury.

Demetrius was matched to fight 2004 US Olympian Vance Martirosyan (33-0-1) for the vacant WBO World Super Welterweight Championship on September 7 at Staples Center in Los Angeles. Andrade vs. Martirosyan finally happened on November 9 in Corpus Christi, Texas. Andrade overcame a flash knockdown in the opening round, using his jab and quickness advantage to take a twelve-round majority decision (117-110, 114-113, 112-115).

The long gaps of inactivity Andrade suffered throughout his pro career, although not necessarily his fault, started in 2014. Because he won a world title that was vacated, "Boo Boo" was forced to fight no. 1 mandatory contender Brian Rose (25-1-1), which didn't happen until June 14, 2014, at Barclays Center in Brooklyn, New York, and it did nothing to enhance Andrade's value because this Rose had already lost his bloom. Andrade simply outclassed his British challenger, landing a straight left hand that dropped Rose in the opening round. A counter right hook dropped Rose in round three, and referee Michael Griffin had seen enough, stepping in to mercifully end the beat down in the seventh round, with Andrade completely dominating the scorecards after six rounds (60-51, 60-52, 60-52). Andrade earned his highest purse to date, $200,000, for his HBO fight versus Rose.

Critics of Andrade jumped on a failed 2014 (December 13) world title fight showdown between undefeated light middleweights Andrade and Jermell Charlo (24-0, 11 KOs), airing on Showtime from Mandalay Bay in Las Vegas. A month before the scheduled fight, alleged purse issues cancelled the fight. What really happened was that Andrade rejected the Charlo fight, believing he had made a deal with Jay-Z's agency, Roc Nation Sports. But the deal fell through when Roc Nation reportedly denied buying out Andrade's contract. Andrade filed suit against Roc

Nation for reneging on an alleged promise to pay him $550,000 to cover the cost of him pulling out of the Charlo fight. Banner Promotions and Star Boxing filed a $20 million lawsuit against Roc Nation for punitive damages, claiming Roc Nation Sports executives interfered with their exclusive promotional contract with Andrade, convincing him to turn down the Charlo fight offer. Undisclosed settlements were made in both lawsuits.

Andrade's growing number of detractors increased their complaints that Andrade talked about fighting the best but that he was all talk, no action. Meanwhile, Andrade was stripped of his WBO title for not defending his title for thirteen months without any scheduled fights. Andrade finally returned to action on October 17, 2015, after sixteen months of inactivity, at Mohegan Sun Arena in Uncasville, Connecticut, against Dario Fabian Pucheta (20-2) for the vacant WBA international light middleweight title. Andrade came out strong, blasting Pucheta to the canvas in round one with a straight left, later in the same round via a right uppercut, and another right ended the fight in the third round.

After fighting only once in 2015, Andrade's lone 2016 fight was held at Turning Stone Resort and Casino in Verona, New York, as part of a Showtime Tripleheader. His opponent was power punching Willie Nelson (25-2-1), who Demetrious floored four times, twice in the final round, for a strong twelve-round technical knockout. Back at the top of boxing's light middleweight food chain, Andrade was now the mandatory challenger for, ironically, newly crowned WBC champion Jermell Charlo, but instead Andrade targeted WBA "super" world champion Erislandy Lara, considered by many as the top dog in the 154-pound division.

Andrade ended up agreeing to fight WBA "regular" champion Jack Culcay (22-1, 11 KOs), who Demetrius had defeated at the 2007 world championships as an amateur. Culcay's promoter, Sauerland Event, won the purse bid, and after a delay the fight happened on March 11, 2017, in Germany, where Andrade won a twelve-round split decision (116-112, 116-112, 114-115) to become world champion once again.

Later, in 2017, Andrade made his middleweight debut in a non-title fight against 23-0-1 Alantez Fox on HBO at Turning Stone. Andrade was dropped in round seven, but otherwise he controlled the fight from start to finish and he was awarded a twelve-round unanimous decision (118-109, 118-110, 116-112).

That following June, Andrade announced he had bought out his contract and his ten-year association with his promoters had ended, and that he was a free agent.

HBO ordered its middleweight champion, Billy Joe Saunders (26-0), to make his mandatory defense against no. 1 rated Andrade, who had signed a promotional contract with newly launched Matchroom Boxing USA, which was changing the way boxing fans viewed the sports, live streaming on DAZN. Andrade was scheduled to challenge Saunders in Boston on October 20, 2018, but Saunders tested positive for a banned substance and the Massachusetts Boxing Commission denied him a license. His title defense was off, and instead Andrade was matched against 17-0 Namibian fighter Walter Kautondokwa, the no. 2 ranked WBO middleweight for the vacant WBO title.

Andrade successfully defended his belt in 2019 by stopping 19-2 Russian Artur Akavov by twelfth round technical knockout, and at home in the Providence Civic Center against Polish challenger Maciej Sulecki (28-1) by manhandling him for a twelve-round unanimous decision in a shutout (120-107 x 3). In his first and only 2020 fight prior to the COVID-19 pandemic, Andrade stopped 17-2-1 Irishman Luke Keeler in the ninth round in Miami.

In 2021, Andrade took a one-sided twelve-round unanimous decision from 23-2-1 Brit challenger Liam Williams in Hollywood, Florida, returning to New England to stop 19-1 Irishman Jason Quigley in Manchester, New Hampshire, in a pair of WBO world title defenses.

Andrade just keeps winning as he looks toward his future.

"When I'm in the gym after I work out," Andrade added, "I'll help some of the other fighters in the gym. After I retire, I will spend time with my family and investments, and I want to travel. I'm already into that (investments) now, not waiting until after I retire like a lot of fighters who end up broke. I would like to help fighters as an advisor, so that they don't get screwed on contracts. I may want to do a little commentating, but not as a career, and only if I could pick and choose when and what fights."

His ability to dominate his opponents, those willing to fight him, shouldn't be held against him. And just maybe, after he's done boxing, in retrospect Demetrious Andrade will finally be more appreciated and valued.

ALL-NEW ENGLAND

Birth Name:	Demetrius Andrade
Nickname:	Boo Boo
Born:	February 26, 1988, in Providence, Rhode Island
Hometown:	Providence, Rhode Island
Amateurs:	200-20, 2008 US Olympian, 2018 World Championship gold medalist, 2005 and 2006 USA National Championships and 2007 National Golden Gloves champion
Pro Record:	31-0 (19 KOs)
Pro Titles:	Two-time WBO super world welterweight (November 9, 2013–July 31, 2015, and March 11, 2017–October 21, 2017), WBO world middleweight (October 20, 2018–present)
Pro Career:	2008–present
Height:	6' 0"
Reach:	73.5"
Stance:	Southpaw
Division:	Middleweight and light middleweight

World Title Fight Record: 9-0 (4 KOs)
Records vs. World Champions: 1-0 (1 KO), defeated Jack Culcay

Manager:	Ed Farris
Trainers:	Paul Andrade, Dave Keefe, Virgil Hunter

Notes: Cape Verdean descent; he has managed and trained a few fighters; as an amateur he traveled the world, competing in China, Russia, and Germany twice apiece, plus Brazil, Venezuela, Hungary, Netherlands, France, and Portugal

No. 19

JACK DELANEY

"Bright Eyes"
Booze, His Toughest Opponent

Smooth in the ring and owning one-punch knockout power in his right hand, the rise and fall of handsome Jack Delaney came relatively swift as alcohol abuse led to his unfortunate demise and subsequent retirement at thirty-two.

Born in Canada, Delaney moved with his family to New England as a child, eventually settling in Bridgeport, Connecticut, and he died at the age of forty-eight in Katonah, New York.

Broken hands nearly ended his career, which commenced in 1919 with a four-round unanimous decision against Steve August, before it really took off. "Bright Eyes"—which he was called because of his marquee looks that attracted female fans called "Delaney's Screaming Mamies"—won thirteen of his first fourteen pro fights with one draw until he lost for the first time on points in a twelve-round match in Providence to 51-32-10 veteran Tommy Robson. A major knockout of 37-3-5 Bert Collins at Ebbets Field in Brooklyn, New York, in seven rounds got him back on the right track to potential stardom.

In 1922, 24-1-1 Delaney defeated 62-9-16 on points in a fifteen-round fight at Casino Hall in Delaney's hometown of Bridgeport to become New England middleweight champion. Two years later, Delaney registered his most notable win to date, decisioning future world light heavyweight champion Tommy Loughran (43-10-4) in their ten-round match at Boston's Mechanic Building.

Up next for Delaney was a sensational fourth-round knockout of previously undefeated Paul Berlenbach at Madison Square Garden. The battle between two feared punchers resulted in Delaney overcoming a knockdown and decking Berlenbach twice in the fourth round, resulting in the referee stopping the fight.

The period between 1924 and 1928 found Delaney as one of boxing's most popular fighters despite losing a pair of six-round bouts on points to his old nemesis, 57-2 Jimmy Slattery. Future world middleweight champion Tiger Flowers (91-11-5) and Delaney had two confrontations in 1925, both held at Madison Square Garden, in which Delaney emerged victorious thanks to second and fourth round stoppages. Their rematch was somewhat bizarre as Delaney floored Flowers with a straight right hand. Flowers was counted out, but his corner protested that it had been a "fast count." On the verge of a riot, Flowers demanded that the fight continue, and Delaney obliged, finishing Flowers off with a vintage right that put Flowers to sleep.

Delaney's reward for defeating Flowers again was a title fight against Berlenbach (28-1-2) at Madison Square Garden. A game Berlenbach managed to out-gut Delaney for a fifteen-round decision. An undaunted Delaney won eleven in a row, including a fourth-round stoppage of Mike McTigue and ten-round decision over Maxie Rosenbloom, positioning Delany for a rematch against NYSAC world light heavyweight champion Berlenbach (31-2-2) at Ebbets Field.

Delaney controlled the fight from start to finish, dropping Berlenbach in the process to win a fifteen-round decision to capture the NYSAC world title on July 16, 1926. Five months later, Delaney successfully defended his strap with a third-round technical knockout of Jamaica Kid. In early 1927, Delaney relinquished his title to move up to the heavyweight ranks, ultimately for a shot at the most coveted individual sports title in the world.

With a title shot on the line to challenge reigning world heavyweight champion Gene Tunney, Delaney was upset by 26-3 Jim Maloney, who took a ten-round unanimous decision at Madison Square Garden.

Delaney's drinking had become a serious detriment at this stage of his career. He was a binge drinker who, unknown to fans and sportswriters, prepared for fights at secluded training camps where liquor was prohibited. Hardly a social drinker, Delaney would often disappear for days on benders, including a three-day disappearing act prior to the Maloney fight. Compounding his behavior was throwing a punch at a railroad porter, who wisely ducked, but Delaney broke his hand striking the steel side of the rail car. Delaney told nobody, including his manager and trainer, and fought Maloney, albeit unable to throw his dreaded right hand.

After a six-month rehabilitation, Delaney returned to the ring on August 11, 1927, when he defeated 29-2-1 Paulino Uzcudun on a seventh-round disqualification at Yankee Stadium. His next fight ended in a ten-round loss on points to dangerous Johnny Risko (40-19-7).

Delaney competed in the first round of famous promoter Tex Rickard's 1928 heavyweight elimination tournament to find an opponent for world heavyweight champion Tunney. Delaney squared off against an opponent who outweighed him by nearly twenty pounds, 65-11-2 Jack Renault, who suffered a broken nose in the fourth round from a crisp Delaney uppercut. Renault bled profusely for the rest of the fight, which "Bright Eyes" won on points. Next won was the fourth encounter between Delaney and 36-5-3 Berlenbach, who had already lost two of their three fights. Delaney closed the show in the sixth round by technical knockout. In 1928, he won four straight fights to improve his record to 71-10-2, earning him a fight with future world heavyweight champion Jack Sharkey (27-8-1).

With another world heavyweight title shot implication on the line against Tunney, Delaney's booze problem reared its ugly head once again, and he entered the ring looking flabby and lacking energy—drunk, according to many. The first bell found him in a near paralyzed state, staring into his corner as Sharkey approached. Sharkey momentarily stalled when he saw Delaney, but he unforgivingly blasted Delaney, flooring him as he embarrassingly went crawling around the ring on his hands and knees as the referee counted him out at the 1:15 mark of the opening round.

For all intents and purposes, Delaney's career was over, although he won three fights by stoppage after his loss to Sharkey.

One can only wonder in retrospect how great Jack Delaney could have been, possibly world heavyweight champion to go with his world light heavyweight title, if not for his toughest opponent: alcohol.

ALL-NEW ENGLAND

Birth Name: Ovila Chapdelaine
Nickname: Bright Eyes
Born: March 18, 1900, in Saint-Francois-du-Luc, Quebec, Canada
Hometown: Bridgeport, Connecticut
Death: November 27, 1948
Pro Record: 73-11-2 (43 KOs, 3 KOBY)
Pro Titles: World light heavyweight champion (July 16, 1926–vacated 1927)
Pro Career: 1919–1932
Height: 5' 11"
Reach: 73.5"
Stance: Orthodox
Division: Heavyweight and light heavyweight

World Title Fight Record: 1-0-1 (1 KO)

Records vs. World Champions: 8-4 (4 KOs, 1 KOBY), defeated Maxie Rosenbloom,* Tommy Loughran,* Paul Berlenbach (thrice), Tiger Flowers (twice), Mike McTigue; lost to Jack Sharkey,* Jimmy Slattery (twice), Paul Berlenbach (* International Boxing HOF)

Manager: Al Jennings, Pete Reilly, Billy Prime

Notes: International Boxing Hall of Fame, Class of 1996; after retiring from the ring, he operated several businesses, including a New York tavern, and he also refereed

No. 20

BATTLING BATTALINO

"Bat"
Super Whiskers

Through eighty-six pro fights and 669 total rounds fought, world featherweight champion Battling Battalino was known respectfully for his granite chin, because he was stopped only once, the result of severe facial cuts that forced the referee to halt the bout.

The future Hall of Fame boxer was a standout amateur who captured top honors at the 1927 National AAU Championships.

A relentless fighter who stalked his opponents, Battalino's pro debut was on June 6, 1927, at the Velodrome in Hartford, Connecticut. Battalino knocked out Archie Rosenberg in the second round. The Italian American fought exclusively in Connecticut for his first twenty-one fights, primarily in Hartford but also in New Haven, Bridgeport, and New Britain. "Bat" won eighteen of these Nutmeg fights with only one loss, one draw, and one no contest.

Battalino established himself during that stretch, including a ten-round victory against future Hall of Famer and NBA world bantamweight champion "Panama" Al Brown (59-7-6) at Bulkeley Stadium in Hartford. His impressive win over Brown positioned him as the no. 1 contender for NBA world featherweight champion André Routis (55-24-7). In front of 13,866 fans at Hurley Stadium in East Hartford, local favorite Battalino was completely dominant, thoroughly

97

outboxing his foe to take all fifteen rounds to become one of the youngest world featherweight champions of all time, as well as Connecticut's first world champion, at the age of twenty-one. Referee Bill Conway was the lone judge who scored the fight in Battalino's favor, 75-56.

Two fights later, Battalino traveled outside of his native Connecticut for the first time as a professional, losing a ten-round unanimous decision to Lew Massey (28-5-4) at the Philadelphia Arena in 1930.

Battalino won the world featherweight championship on July 15, 1930, when he stopped Filipino challenger Ignacio Fernandez (31-21-10) at Hurley Stadium in the fifth round, marking the first time Fernandez had been knocked out during his career.

In 1931, Battalino faced his own version of "Murder's Row" in that era: defeating 112-28-15 Bud Taylor (DEC10) and 57-2-1 Kid Chocolate (57-2-1) for the New York State (NYSAC) world featherweight title; losing to 51-12-7 Cecil Payne (DEC10), 37-7-2 Roger Bernard (PTS10), 105-19-16 Louis "Kid" Kaplan (PTS10), and 28-9-2 Young Zazzarino (DQ3).

By this point it was apparent that Battalino would fight any opponent who had the courage to step up those three steps into the ring. Battalino hadn't received proper respect as a world champion though, largely due to the relatively weak challengers he had defeated in title fights. In 1931, he finally earned respect against 2-1 favorite Fidel LaBarba (48-8-7), the 1924 Olympic gold medalist in the flyweight division, winning a conclusive fifteen-round decision at Madison Square Garden in their NYSAC world featherweight championship bout.

Two fights and two months later, Battalino successfully defended his NBA and world featherweight titles in Cincinnati, taking a ten-round unanimous decision from 86-4-3 Freddie Miller. He bounced back from back to back non-title fight losses to 93-18-3 Bushy Graham, the former world bantamweight champion, and 46-11-3 Roger Bernard, with a ten-round majority decision over 49-3-2 Earl Mastro in Chicago to defend his NBA and world featherweight titles. "Bat" followed with first and second round knockouts, respectively, of Graham in their rematch and 58-8-2 Al Singer.

Miller challenged Battalino again for his crowns in a boring 1932 match in Cincinnati that ended controversially with Battalino—who had already lost recognition as world champion because he weighed in three and three-quarter pounds more than the 126-pound limit—dropped twice in the third round, both on questionable punches, and referee Lou Bauman halted the fight on the advice of the Cincinnati Boxing Commission. The fight was ruled a "No Contest." Ticket holders were given their money back. Battalino was fined and suspended, and his title was the original world featherweight championship ever abandoned in the history of Madison Square Garden.

Later, in 1932, Battalino went through a four-fight losing streak, two each to the Petrolle brothers. "Bat" was stopped for the first and only time as a prizefighter on March 24, 1932, at Madison Square Garden by future Hall of Famer Billy Petrolle (116-23-14) in front of a reported 18,000 fans. Ripping rights and lefts caused a dozen bleeding cuts to Battalino's face. Two vicious rights signaled the end, but the incredibly tough Battalino refused to go down after a fuselage of punches, and referee Gunboat Smith halted the action and awarded Petrolle the fight via a technical knockout.

In a rematch two months later in Chicago, Battalino rocked Petrolle with a well-placed left hook that sent Petrolle to the canvas. He beat the count at nine and survived until he gathered himself. Petrolle triumphed by winning seven of the ten rounds for a win by unanimous decision. Battalino didn't have any more success with Petrolle's brother, Frankie (27-22-12), in a pair of losses by decision in Long Island City in Queens, New York.

Battalino won six of his next nine fights, including a loss by ten-round decision to 37-2-2 Barney Ross. He then destroyed an overmatched 56-16-3 Cocoa Kid, who was an intra-state rival fighting at a lower weight. Battalino beat Kid from pillar to post until Kid, who was visibly no longer able to raise his arms to defend himself, retired after eight rounds at Food Guard Hall in Hartford.

Battling Battalino may have had the best whiskers in boxing based on him being stopped only once—and that on cuts—against a who's who list of opponents during his thirteen-year pro career.

ALL-NEW ENGLAND

Birth Name:	Christopher Battaglia
Nickname:	Bat
Born:	February 18, 1908, in Hartford, Connecticut
Hometown:	Hartford, Connecticut
Death:	July 25, 1977
Amateurs:	1927 National AA champion
Pro Record:	57-26-3 (23 KOs, 1 KOBY)
Pro Titles:	World featherweight champion
Pro Career:	1927–1940
Height:	5' 5.5"
Reach:	65"
Stance:	Orthodox
Division:	Featherweight, lightweight

World Title Fight Record: 4-0 1 NC (0 KOs)

Records vs. World Champions: 8-4 (2 KOs, 0 KOBY), defeated Fidel LaBarba,* Freddie Miller,* Panama Brown,* Andre Routis, Kid Chocolate,* Bushy Graham (twice), Al Singer, Bud Taylor*; lost to Barney Ross,* Louis "Kid" Kaplan,* Bud Taylor,* Bushy Graham (* International Boxing HOF)

Manager: Hy Malley, Lenny Marello

Notes: International Boxing Hall of Fame, Class of 2003; son of Italian immigrants; never attended high school, quitting school in fifth grade, and he worked in a typewriter factory and in tobacco fields; rescued a drowning three-year-old in Park River, for which he received a Connecticut Humane Society award for his courage; became a construction worker after he retired from boxing and helped build the Hartford Civic Center

No. 21

COCOA KID

Triple Threat

Although he never captured a legitimate world title, Cocoa Kid fought the best fighters of his era for nineteen years (1929–48) despite limited opportunities because he was of African descent and white world champions were notoriously reluctant to fight black opponents.

Cocoa Kid's toughest fight may have happened long before he ever laced up a pair of boxing gloves. Born in Puerto Rico to his native mother Maria Arroyo and Lewis Hardwick, an African American merchant marine who left Puerto Rico without realizing that Maria was pregnant until his return several months later. Kid Cocoa, born Herbert Lewis Hardwick Arroyo, moved as a child to Atlanta.

In 1918, Hardwick's father and the rest of the USS *Cyclops* crew perished during World War I without a trace, the single largest loss of life in US naval history; 306 crew and passengers, excluding combat involvement, and the cause was unknown. Hardwick was only four years old, and soon afterward, upon the death of his mother, Hardwick lived in Atlanta with his maternal aunt, Antonio Arroyo-Robinson.

Hardwick stared boxing when he was fourteen, his first fight coming the following year. In 1932, Connecticut State Senator Harry Durant attended one of Hardwick's amateur fights in West Palm Beach, Florida. He was so impressed by Hardwick that he sponsored a trip to New Haven, Connecticut, where Hardwick fought under the pseudonym "Kid Cocoa," and resided the rest of his life

His first pro fight was on May 27, 1929, in Atlanta, where he defeated Kid Moon on points in eight rounds. Kid Cocoa's arduous journey continued for nearly two decades until he retired in 1948 with a 178-58-11 pro record.

In 1933, he won a pair of significant fights against world champions, 120-22-16 Louis "Kid" Kaplan and 81-22-5 Johnny Jadick, both by points in ten-round matches to prove himself on a national scale. Cocoa Kid took on all comers, and in 1933–34 he unsuccessfully took on 26-0-3 Lou Ambers (PTS10), and fighting at a lower weight, 46-20-2 Battling Battalino (RTD6) in 1933–34. The next year he knocked out Andy Callahan in round ten to become the New England welterweight champion when the New England champion really meant something, as opposed to the unsanctioned New England champions of the twenty-first century.

Kid Cocoa paid the price for being a black boxer during the late thirties and early forties when top rated and champion white boxers refused to fight black opponents. Kid Cocoa was joined by Charley Burley, Holman Williams, Jack Chase, Lloyd Marshall, Bert Lytell, and Eddie Booker in the "Black Murders Row." They were the most avoided fighters in the world, forced to repeatedly fight each other. Kid Cocoa, for example, fought Williams thirteen times (8-3-2).

During most of 1940, Kid Cocoa was the world's no. 1 welterweight contender, but fellow black, the reigning world welterweight champion, Henry Armstrong refused to give Cocoa Kid a world title shot.

In 1936, the world colored welterweight title was created, and Cocoa Kid defeated 53-9-4 Young Peter Jackson by way of a second-round technical knockout to become its first champion. Cocoa Kid made four title defenses, winning three and losing to Charlie Burley, later decisioning old rival Williams for the World Colored Middleweight Championship.

From 1939 through 1940, Kid Cocoa reeled off seventeen consecutive victories, highlighted by a ten-round majority decision win versus 108-27-17 Chalky Wright, along with points victories versus 125-20-14 Jimmy Leto and 119-59-20 Bill McDowell.

Kid Cocoa finally got his world title shot in 1940, albeit only the Maryland version, in Baltimore with the great Jack Dempsey serving as referee. When the final bell sounded after fifteen rounds, Izzy Jannazzo (35-10-13) squeaked out a split decision win.

In 1944, Cocoa Kid found himself in the center of controversy at the Civic Center in San Francisco against 18-9-3 "Oakland" Billy Smith. Four times Kid Cocoa was knocked down from punches considered by referee Frankie Brown as not hard enough to result in a knockdown, and he stopped the fight in the third, declaring it a "no contest." The California Boxing Commission investigated the fight. Kid Cocoa had been a solid 2-1 favorite, and it withheld his purse, issued a $500 fine, and suspended him for six months. Kid Cocoa claimed his subpar performance was due to anxiety involving his sick aunt who had brought him up, but the commission felt that he was throwing the fight.

Kid Cocoa, who used the entire ring as his stage because of his dazzling footwork, effectively snapping a stiff left jab to set up his dangerous right hand, may never had been a recognized as a world champion, but remarkably he was a top ten contender in three different weight classes: lightweight, welterweight, and middleweight.

ALL-NEW ENGLAND

Birth Name: Herbert Lewis Hardwick
Nickname: Cocoa Kid
Born: May 2, 1914, in Mayaguez, Puerto Rico
Hometown: New Haven, Connecticut
Death: December 27, 1929
Amateurs: 1938–39 Connecticut state champion
Pro Record: 178-58-11 (48 KOs, 7 KOBY)
Pro Career: 1940–66
Height: 5' 10.5"
Stance: Orthodox
Division: Lightweight, welterweight, and middleweight

World Title Fight Record: 0-1 (1 KOBY)
Records vs. World Champions: 3-6-1 (0 KOs, 2 KOBY), defeated Louis Kid Kaplan,* Chalky Wright,* Johnny Jadick; lost to Charley Burley,* Battling Battalino,* Lou Ambers,* Izzy Jannazzo(twice), Archie Moore*; draw with Charley Burley* (* International Boxing HOF)

Manager: Walter Travers, Pete Reilly
Trainer: Sammy Shack, Lou Caroby, Bernie Bernstein

Notes: International Boxing Hall of Fame, Class of 2012; he served in the US Navy during World War II and was honorably discharged with pugilistic dementia, which he had kept secret for years as a boxer

No. 22

TRAVIS SIMMS

"Tremendous"
Twin Peaks

Two-time world junior middleweight champion "Tremendous" Travis Simms is one-half of arguably the most prolific twin-brother tandem in boxing history. He and his twin brother, "Marvelous" Marvin Simms, combined for a 55-2-1 (30 KOs) professional record during their careers from 1997 to 2014.

Boxing brothers in the pro ranks are relatively rare, and twin brothers, to say the least, are extremely unusual. The Simms twins are inarguably the best pair in New England boxing history since the world champion Sullivan twins (welterweight Mike and light heavyweight Jack) ruled the ring back in the early years of the twentieth century. Both of the Sullivans used the nickname "Twin," and were born in Cambridge (MA) and later lived in Boston.

The Simms twins started boxing when they were five, introduced to the sport at the Meadow Gardens Boxing Club in their hometown of Norwalk, Connecticut. They never switched places or even joked about it, yet at more than one weigh-in a trainer claimed that their boxer was supposed to fight the other twin.

"No, we never even joked about it, but that's because we fought in different weight classes (156 lbs.)," Travis explained. "As novices, we were fighting in the same weight class, but we flipped a coin to see

105

who would fight at 156 or 165. I won and stayed at 156, he (Marvin) went up to 165. We won the Golden Gloves Regionals, I made it to the finals, my brother won the 1988 Nationals, in Little Rock, Arkansas."

Unlike many boxers, Travis enjoyed being from New England, and he successfully took the challenge of training in the cold and snow during winters. "I loved it," Simms proclaimed. "I found the air to be much fresher and cleaner in the cold and it pushed me. My favorite fight I had in New England was in the New England Golden Gloves in my first opportunity to go and compete in Lowell (MA). Winning the Golden Gloves was my most memorable fight. I went on to the Regionals and represented our region at the USA Championships."

Travis Simms (28-1, 19 KOs) was a highly decorated amateur boxer, whose long-anticipated pro debut was February 10, 1998, in Baton Rouge, Louisiana, when he stopped Michael Brown in three rounds. Simms fought six times in 1998 and again in 1999. In 2000, the southpaw faced his first real test of his then sixteen-fight pro career, 25-6-3 Kevin Kelly, who lost an eight-round unanimous decision.

Simms was fed a steady diet of journeymen, building his record to 21-0, going into his November 1, 2002, fight versus 26-5-1 Anton Robinson for the vacant NABA super welterweight title. Simms recorded a win by seventh-round knockout, setting the stage for his first world title fight on December 13, 2003, against undefeated defending WBA super welterweight world champion Alejandro Garcia at Boardwalk Hall in Atlantic City, New Jersey.

In the battle of undefeated fighters with identical 22-0 pro records airing on HBO pay-per-view, Simms knocked out Garcia in the fifth round, and he returned home to Norwalk a world champion and a conquering hero.

"Garcia had knocked out Santiago Samaniego to win the vacated WBA (Junior Welterweight) title when they elevated Mosley to Super champ," Simms remembered. "I signed with Don King to get a fight with Garcia, but Garcia signed to fight Rhoshii Wells in Connecticut at Mohegan Sun. I was supposed to fight on the undercard, but my opponent wasn't seen after the weigh in. Wells led in the fight, but he was knocked out in the 10th round. I thought I'd be fighting Wells.

Garcia was 27-0 with 27 knockouts, but he wasn't well known. So, he had good power and I worked with heavy-handed fighters during training camp. They said they'd make the fight with Garcia in Atlantic City on pay per view. I had the flu and two broken hands going into the fight. I trained in the Poconos. Once I got to Atlantic City, I felt sick. I felt ill with the chills and irritable. I was full blown sick and tried to hide it from the doctors. At 3 in the morning, my team got me some medicine, and I must have finished the bottle in an hour. I felt better and said I'd take it again an hour before my pre-fight physical.

"When the doctor was checking my hands, they squeezed 'em and I wanted to scream because it hurt so much. They said I was good to go. My trainers wanted me to pull out of the fight, but I said no way, I'm fighting for the title. It was amazing to go through all that and come out victoriously. I dominated the first four rounds, but then the medicine started kicking in. Then he hit me so hard with a right that it woke me up. I said to myself that I couldn't let him hit me again. I'd never been hit that hard, like I was hit by King Kong. Instead of getting knocked out, I woke up, and in the fifth round I started boxing and was super alert. I hit him and saw that his legs buckled. I got closer to him and noticed that he was out on his feet. He was hurt. I put my hands against his chest and before the referee came in to break us up, I hit him with a short, 6-inch punch. I threw the perfect punch, right on his chin, and he didn't get up."

Norwalk City officials proclaimed January 13, 2014 as Travis Simms Day, and that evening he attended the Norwalk Common Council meeting, where a resolution was passed renaming a street where he grew up in the South Norwalk neighborhood as Travis Simms Way. Two weeks later, the City of Norwalk paid tribute to the new world champion, only the seventh in Connecticut history, with a celebration dinner honoring him.

Becoming world champion and the notoriety that goes along with fame naturally changed his life in a positive manner.

"I'd do it all over the same way," Simms said. "I have no regrets about my career. Some things I wish I had done better, but I'm so fortunate to be world champion. My life changed almost immediately, the way people looked at me and treated me differently. A whole new life opened up; I was invited to social events, private gatherings and I had endless exposure to a class of celebrities and high-ranking politicians. As fast as it came, it goes fast when you are world champion, but it means the world to me because of what I overcame in life. I sacrificed so much for many years. I was so committed to being a champion; hard to explain but it drove me. I never cut corners and was dedicated to my craft. I stayed in the gym and from my early to mid-twenties, I drove to New York City to get better training and sparring. Seven days a week! My wife worked, so every day I took the kids with me to the gym. I felt sick if I didn't run and train. My ritual was to get up at 4 or 5 a.m. and run 3, 8 or more miles. I ran so early because there wouldn't be cars on the road when I ran. I took ownership of that."

Later that year, Simms made his first title defense against former world champion Bronco McKart (47-5), featured on another HBO pay-per-view, at famed Madison Square Garden. Simms won a fairly one-sided twelve-round unanimous decision (118-110, 117-111, 116-112).

Two months after being crowned, Simms' lawyer, Kurt Emhoff, contacted WBA executive Renzo Bagnariol to ask for a clarification about when Simms, the WBA "regular" junior welterweight world titlist, would be able to challenge the WBA "super" light middleweight champion. An email from the WBA clearly stated that Simms would be able to fight the winner of the March 13, 2004 unification fight between WBA "super" champion Shane Mosley (who had beaten Oscar de la Hoya twice) and IBF title-holder Ronald "Winky" Wright (who won a twelve-round unanimous decision).

Bagnariol confirmed the WBA's mandate four days prior to Wright vs. Mosley, but only three weeks later the WBA informed Atty. Emhoff that Simms' mandatory would be delayed due to a WBA rule change.

In violation of its own rules, Wright was allowed to fight Mosley in a rematch that the defending champion won; however, Simms reportedly received word from the WBA that he may have to make two title defenses before the WBA would order the Wright-Simms title fight.

"Now," Simms noted, "I was champion and I wanted to unify. King wanted the rematch with Garcia. I wanted to fight the guys who wouldn't fight me. Even though I had signed with King, Don said he'd get me a fight with Felix Trinidad, but first Winky Wright knocked him out. Wright didn't have any power; I would have destroyed him (Trinidad). I believed I could beat anybody in the world. The WBC and King wanted me fight Garcia again, but I refused until after I had fought one of the big champs. They stripped me and had Garcia fight Jose Rivera for the title."

The WBA stripped Simms of his title on March 20, 2005. Simms filed a lawsuit in federal court seeking unspecified damages and injunctive relief requiring the WBA to follow its rules by ordering Wright-Simms, and if Wright refused the bout, Simms wanted him stripped off his super champion status just as the WBA had recently done to its "super" junior welterweight champion Kosta Tszyu.

An out-of-court settlement was reached during August 2006, in which Simms was matched against fellow New Englander WBA "regular" champion Jose Antonio Rivera. Simms, though, was inactive for two and a half years without a payday. It didn't matter, because eventually Simms recaptured the WBA after being reinstated as the WBA "Champion in Recess," and mandatory challenger Simms captured the WBA super welterweight world title with a ninth-round knockout of Rivera live on Showtime from Seminole Hard Rock in Hollywood, Florida.

Simms' second reign as WBA junior middleweight world champion, as well as his perfect record, were snapped on July 7, 2007, in Simms' title defense against undefeated Canadian challenger Joachim Alcine (28-0). Simms lost his belt and undefeated record to Alcine by way of a twelve-round unanimous decision (116-109, 115-110, 114-111) in Simms' homecoming at Arena at Harbor Yard in Bridgeport, Connecticut.

Boxing politics had ultimately sapped Simms' passion for boxing. He only fought three more times against Mike McFail (WDEC6) in 2008, Marcus Luck (WTKO3) in 2009, and Jess Noriega (WDEC6) in 2014, when Simms fought as a light heavyweight five years after his earlier fight.

"It was all about boxing politics," Simms commented on the dark side of boxing he experienced. "I was No. 1 in the WBC and WBA.

I was the mandatory challenger for the regular title. They came up with Super champion. We called it the Simms Rule, implemented the change, and upgraded Oscar de la Hoya and then Shane Mosley to Super Champion. All the top fighters avoided me, and I understood why. I had power, speed, and agility. The WBC ignored me. The WBA matched me against Kevin Kelly in an eliminator and I destroyed him. He was highly rated, and we wanted to fight him in the eliminator, because defeating him would put me No. 1 across the board. I signed with Don King to fight the Super champion, I believe Mosley or Vargas, at that time."

Simms may have retired from the ring, but his experiences—good and bad—hardened him for the next chapter of his life as a politician. An advocate of Norwalk's poor and minority residents, Simms understands their needs because he's been there himself.

The tough lessons he learned in boxing has aided him in the Connecticut House of Representatives, where he represents the 140th Assembly District in Norwalk's center district.

"I never thought I'd be a state rep," Simms concluded. "I was a Norwalk City Councilor, and the opportunity came to run for state representative in District 4, where I was born and lived. I knew the issues and policies in place and wanted to do something. I grew up in a housing project, the youngest of 8 children. I was a kid without resources who became world champion. I wanted to bridge the disparity for those considered low income or poor. I'm still learning the ropes and I'm focused on being a state rep.

"Boxing helped prepared me to be a state rep. Learning how to speak at press conferences and in interviews helped me speak as a politician. Boxing showed me how to be disciplined and that's helped in negotiations with colleagues across the aisle. I did look at my contracts (when he fought) to the point it was almost like I'm an attorney. The skill sets and patience I've carried from boxing to politics has helped me. By far, though, politics is a lot tougher than boxing. You don't know who your opponents are and it's challenging to take people at their word or face value. I represent more than my family and friends. I need to represent my constituents in Hartford.

"I've always been a fan, I love boxing. It's my life. Boxing today is exciting. More importantly, fights are competitive, and fighters have more control of their careers and are better paid. Fighters today are more than fighters; they are businessmen and businesswomen. I still go to the gym, and I do own a boxing promotional company, but Covid has hurt the boxing industry, and with me now being a state rep, I haven't been able to put on any shows."

Whether in the ring or statehouse, Travis Simms has been "Tremendous" and a true fighter.

ALL-NEW ENGLAND

Birth Name:	Travis Simms
Nickname:	Tremendous
Born:	May 1, 1971, in Norwalk, Connecticut
Hometown:	Norwalk, Connecticut
Amateurs:	295-10, 1995 National PAL champion, four-time New England champion, 1997 New York Golden Gloves champion, and Sugar Ray Robinson Award winner as Best Boxer of the Tournament
Pro Record:	28-1 (19 KOs, 0 KOBY)
Pro Titles:	Two-time World Boxing Association light middleweight world champion (December 13, 2003–June 2005; In Recess August 2006–January 6, 2007, January 1, 2007–July 7, 2017)
Pro Career:	1998–2014
Height:	5' 9.5"
Reach:	69"
Stance:	Southpaw
Division:	Junior middleweight

World Title Fight Record: 3-1 (2 KOs, 0 KOBY)
Records vs. World Champions: 3-0 (2 KOs), defeated Jose Antonio Rivera, Bronco McKart, Alejandro Garcia; lost to Joachim Alcine

Manager:	Sandra Simms
Trainer:	Nirmal Lorick

Notes: Simms was the no. 1 alternate to 1996 US Olympian David Reid, the lone American to capture a gold medal that year; a proud African American, Simms' great-grandmother was Cherokee Indian

No. 23

JOSE ANTONIO RIVERA

"El Gallo"
Working Class World Champion

Most world boxing champions do not work full-time jobs. They live off their purse earnings and hope through investments that it lasts a lifetime, especially if they have large families. Two-division world champion "El Gallo" Jose Antonio Rivera was clearly the exception.

Rivera was an associate court officer for the Commonwealth of Massachusetts Trial Courts, and was promoted in 2019 to assistant chief court officer in his hometown of Worcester, Massachusetts. He used his vacation time, as well as personal and sick days, to be able to train properly for some of his major fights. Jose understood that boxing wasn't going to last forever, and when he became a father for the first time at the age of twenty, one year after he turned pro, the need for a steady paycheck, benefits, and retirement became crucial for him.

Like many prizefighters, Rivera was saved by boxing (and he's the first to admit it) because he was on his own at an early age and heading down the wrong path. Born in Philadelphia, Jose lived in Puerto Rico and then Springfield, Massachusetts, prior to him moving to Worcester, where he fortunately met a man who helped alter his life: Carlos Garcia, the director in charge of a special boxing program at the Worcester Boys and Girls Club for kids in need of guidance and direction. Alone at the age of sixteen, he moved into an apartment with his friend and four-time national amateur champion Bobby Harris, who went on to post a 20-2-1 (13 KOs) pro record as a heavyweight.

Rivera had started boxing at the age of fourteen and a half in a basement with his friend Felix Lopez, falling in love with boxing after watching Roberto Duran upset "Sugar" Ray Leonard in their first fight. The young Puerto Rican-American specifically used his amateur boxing experience to prepare for the professional ranks. Garcia, who is in the National Golden Gloves Hall of Fame, put him in a novice match after only one amateur fight in order to get Rivera on the fast track, because he understood that Rivera dreamed of becoming world champion as a professional. Rivera finished his amateur career with a 35-15 record, highlighted by a bronze medal performance at the PAL Nationals.

"Growing up when I was in the amateurs," Rivera said, "I was told New England-based boxers do not get much respect compared to boxers who came from New York, New Jersey, Philadelphia, Los Angeles, etc. I used that as motivation when I was able to represent New England on the national stage, amateur or pro. I wanted them to know boxers from New England are talented and tough. I am proud to be part of this elite group of New England boxers that have been able to stand out, proudly representing New England.

"I trained in New England pretty much for most of my boxing career. As a pro there were times when I would travel out of state for training camps. My favorite story was when I was training in Texas, trying to impress Lou Duva. I was hoping to earn a spot in the Main Events stable. I was 1-0 as a pro and they were more interested in a heavyweight from Worcester, Bobby Harris, Jr., who was an amateur standout, a 4-time National Champion who made it to the final of Olympic Box-Offs. I had the pleasure to spar the great Pernell Whitaker that week. This was right before he started getting ready for his Julio Cesar Chavez fight. It was between me and another welterweight they were looking at and we split rounds sparring with Whitaker. I don't remember his name, but he must have impressed them more than me because I never got signed. Yeah, I took that personally and added that to my motivation. Trainer Ronnie Shields was helping us out and in Whitaker's corner was legendary trainer George Benton. When

Whitaker was sparring the other kid, I was standing by Whitaker's corner absorbing all of Benton's instructions like a sponge. Then it was my time to go in the ring. I am not going to say Whitaker was going all out on me, I'm smarter than that, but I know I earned his respect when he asked Ronnie for an extra round, after I blew my load in what I thought was the final round. Ronnie looked at me and asked if that was okay and I said, 'Hell, yeah!' How many times is a 1-0 kid going to get the chance to spar a legend like Pernell Whitaker? Let's just say Whitaker did not use that round to try and abuse me. He pulled out some of his defensive tactics that had me swinging at air. I laughed, he laughed, because the point was well taken. He just wanted to show me that I was not in his league."

Rivera may not have been in the same class as Whitaker, but the rugged "El Gallo" went on to have a terrific pro career, becoming the first Massachusetts fighter in modern history to capture world titles in two different weight classes.

Rivera continued, "When I first started boxing I had the right mindset. My talent was decent, but I was hungry, motivated, and committed to my dream of becoming a world champion boxer. I just needed the right trainer who would give me the opportunity to follow my dream. I found Carlos Garcia who had a good group of amateurs in his boxing stable at the iconic Worcester Boys & Girls Club. I lived in Springfield (MA) at the time, and I was not active as far as fights went, but I was always in the gym learning my craft. While visiting my sisters and younger brother in Worcester, they showed me newspaper clippings of the great things Carlos was doing with the youth at the Boys & Girls Club. The first thought that came to my mind was that I needed to be part of that. At 16 years old, I finished my sophomore year of high school and decided to move to Worcester on my own to go after my dream. Throughout our travels to gyms and fights in New England, Carlos would share stories of how great certain boxers could have been, if it not for drugs, the streets, girls, lack of dedication, need of money or whatever, something stopped these boxers from getting to the next level. I refused to let that happen to me. A lot of time, boxers would train 9 months out of the year and enjoy summers. I trained year-round and had no problem missing birthdays, holidays, and parties. I remember blossoming at 18 years old, starting to develop some punch on my punches. I only had one fight in the novice division. At 16, I competed against 25-32-year-old boxers with more experience. Once I could see my growth and improvement, I developed my motto and have been living it ever since: Believe in Yourself, Work Hard, Never Give up!"

On November 7, 1992, Rivera made his pro debut, knocking out Francisco Mercedes in the second round. He went on to win his first twenty-three pro bouts, including the Massachusetts State welterweight title in 1995. His first pro loss was to veteran Philadelphia fighter Willie Wise (20-3-4), who won a controversial ten-round split decision at Foxwoods Resort Casino in Connecticut. Rivera had proven that he was more than a prospect in his first loss, dropping a close decision (98-95, 94-97, 94-96) to an opponent who went on to upset Mexican icon Julio Cesar Chavez (102-3-2) only three years later.

Showing the same resiliency that stayed with Rivera throughout his entire career, two fights later "El Gallo" stopped Gilberto Flores in two rounds to capture the International Boxing Organization (IBO) world welterweight championship. Rivera extended his new win streak to seven before losing back to back fights. Four fights later, though, Rivera registered his first statement victory in 2001, knocking out three-time world super welterweight champion Frankie Randall (55-10-1) in the tenth round to keep his NABA crown in his first defense.

Promoted by legendary Don King when he traveled across the Atlantic Ocean in September 2003 to Germany, where few Americans were ever able to win, Rivera proved early that he was serious, dropping previously undefeated Michel Trabant in the second round en route to winning a twelve-round majority decision for the vacant WBA. His reign, unfortunately, didn't last long.

Rivera was supposed to cash in on April 17, 2004, earning the highest purse of his career by far, $250,000, against high-profile challenger Ricardo "El Matador" Mayorga at Madison Square Garden. Mayorga weighed in for the title fight at 153.5 pounds, 6.5 more than the contracted weight for their world title fight. Rivera quickly learned about boxing's dark side when he turned down the opportunity to fight for considerably less money against an overweight Mayorga in a non-title fight. Even though it was the challenger, not the defending champion who came in overweight, Rivera was bumped from the card because a new purse and weight agreement wasn't sufficient enough for Rivera. Meanwhile, the foul-mouthed Nicaraguan Mayorga was rewarded with a considerably weaker opponent than Rivera, 16-3-1 Eric Mitchell, for a boring fight that Mayorga won by decision.

Inactive from September 13, 2003, when he captured the WBA world welterweight title, to April 2, 2005, Rivera lost a twelve-round split decision (115-113, 113-115, 113-115) to challenger Luis Collazo (24-1) in Worcester.

Regarding the Mayorga fiasco, justice eventually prevailed, albeit for a much smaller purse for Rivera, who moved up one weight class as the challenger for his next fight (May 6, 2006) in front of 9,000 fans at the DCU Center in Worcester. Displaying the same fire and tenacity that was a staple during his entire career for his next fight, Rivera pounded WBA world junior middleweight champion Alexandro Garcia (25-1), decking him five times and overcoming a fourth-round knockdown for a title-winning twelve-round unanimous decision (116-106, 116-106) 114-107).

In his next fight and first defense of his WBA junior middleweight title belt, Rivera was stopped for the first time in his pro career by new champion Travis Simms (24-0) to open 2007, and then he was knocked out by Daniel Santos (24-0) in round eight of their WBA junior middleweight title eliminator nine months later.

Rivera retired in 2008, only to make a comeback a year later. After which he retired again until returning for two fights in Worcester to complete his pro career with fifty fights, the last coming at the age of forty-six. He retired with a 43-6-1 (25 KOs) pro record.

A true New Englander, even though technically he wasn't born in the six-state area, Rivera has always felt at home in Worcester, where he remains a sports hero.

"Aside from going to a few training camps during my professional career," Rivera concluded, "I just found training at home suited me best. I enjoyed some of the training camps I attended out of state, but I always felt I was one of the boxers that didn't feel training at home was a distraction. I was too focused."

Jose Antonio Rivera will be best known for his toughness, determination, and class in the squared ring, which led him to become a two-division world champion in addition to a wonderful life he never would have enjoyed if had quit his job, even though he never did cash out like he would have if not for the lost money from the Mayorga fiasco.

ALL-NEW ENGLAND

Birth Name:	Jose Antonio Rivera
Nickname:	El Gallo
Born:	April 7, 1973, in Philadelphia, Pennsylvania
Hometown:	Worcester, Massachusetts
Amateurs:	35-15, PAL Nationals bronze medalist
Pro Record:	43-6-1 (25 KOs), 2 KOBY
Pro Titles:	WBA world welterweight champion (September 23, 2003–April 2, 2005), WBA world light middleweight champion (May 6, 2006–January 6, 2007)
Pro Career:	1992–2019
Height:	5' 8"
Reach:	70"
Stance:	Orthodox
Division:	Welterweight and light middleweight

World Title Fight Record: 2-2 (0 KOs, 1 KOBY)
Records vs. World Champions: 2-3 (1 KO, 2 KOBY), defeated Frankie Randall, Alejandro Garcia; lost to Luis Collazo, Travis Simms, Daniel Santos

Trainer: Rocky Gonzalez

Notes: First Latino World Champion and first two-division world champion in Massachusetts boxing history; Rivera and his oldest son, A. J. Rivera, own and run a boxing promotional company, Rivera Promotions Entertainment, to give young fighters from their Worcester hometown opportunities to fight more often and at home

No. 24

JOEY GAMACHE

The Maine Outlier

Maine is known for its succulent lobster, nutritious blueberries, and rocky coastline. And let's not forget, it's also the home of native son Stephen King, the preeminent author of horror books.

Nobody ever mentions boxing and Maine in the same breath. The reason is that the most northeast state in the United States has produced only one world boxing champion, Joey Gamache, who was born in Bath and raised in Lewiston—infamous as the site of the controversial Muhammad Ali vs. Sonny Liston II World Heavyweight Championship match in 1965.

The story goes that Gamache got into boxing because he was a youth third baseman who looped his throws to first base. Gamache's father recommended that his son workout at a boxing gym to strengthen his arm. It wasn't too long before Gamache was hooked on the "Sweet Science," and his days playing on a baseball diamond was history.

Gamache went on to become a decorated amateur boxer who at one point was ranked no. 1 in the United States and no. 3 in the world. He was a multiple national champion, but his bid to make the 1984 US Olympic Boxing Team was unsuccessful, as he settled for a bronze medal at the US Olympic Trials in the 132-pound lightweight division. Wrong year for Gamache to compete in that weight class because Pernell Whitaker went on to win an Olympic gold medal after Joey had lost to Joe Belinc in the semifinals of the Olympic Trials.

"Coming from Maine," Gamache commented, "I saw fights a long time ago. There wasn't a lot of prospect development in Maine, but my goal was never to turn pro. I started boxing at 9. I remember going to Memorial Auditorium in Lowell (MA) for a tournament. I wanted to fight there. Boston was the big place back then for boxing, but the New England Golden Gloves in Lowell was big for amateurs. There were so many good amateurs there, I remember David Attardo. Me, Vinny Paz, and Micky Ward lost to him, but he didn't make it as a pro (1-0). My father, Joe Sr., promoted shows in Maine that built up my name. He had the Golden Gloves franchise there. I was a big-ticket seller. He never wanted to promote pro shows, but it helped being marketable to get on television. Having a good team was huge. They say it takes 3 years to make a champion and only 3 seconds to lose. I was No. 1 in the country, No. 4 in the world, at one point. I finished third at the Olympic Trials, and the National Golden Gloves and Junior Olympic champion. I had good success as an amateur."

Gamache made his successful pro debut on May 1, 1987, in Lewiston, taking his first pro victory when his opponent, Al Jackson, retired after the third of a scheduled six-round match. Joey went on to win his first twenty-nine pro fights to become a local sports hero. In his twenty-fifth pro fight, Gamache scored a tenth round knockout of 19-1 Jerry Ngobeni in Lewiston to capture the vacant WBU Super Featherweight World Championship. Gamache vacated the title, and four fights later, Joey won the vacant WBA world lightweight title, stopping 18-1 Chil Sung Jun at Cumberland Civic Center in Portland, Maine.

Gamache's undefeated streak was snapped in his first title defense four months after his title reign started, when he ran out of gas and was knocked out in the eleventh round by 40-3-1 Tony Lopez at Cumberland Civic Center. Gamache had been ahead on two judges' scorecards and deadlocked on the other card going into the eleventh round. A bloodied and tiring Gamache was dropped in the eleventh. Although he beat the count, referee James Santa halted the fight.

The following year, Gamache reeled off seven victories, including a tenth round knockout of 31-7-1 Jeff Bumpus and twelfth round stoppage of 23-4-2 Jeff Mayweather for the vacant NABF crown, setting up Gamache's 1994 against of 19-0 World Boxing Association (WBA) Orzubek Nazarov in Portland. Gamache got caught early and he never recovered. He was decked twice, and put to sleep in the second round.

The resilient Gamache won his next seven fights on his way to challenging WBU super lightweight world champion Rocky Martinez (20-1), whose only pro loss until then had been to IBF lightweight world champion Phillip Holiday. Gamache won a twelve-round unanimous decision in Portland.

"In the end," Gamache said, "I moved to New York City to get more experience. I didn't have the competition like fighters from other places. Why not New York City instead of going out to the West Coast in California or Vegas? I wanted to develop as a fighter and trainer by learning the sport of boxing."

Two fights later, Gamache stepped up in terms of facing quality opponents, but he lost in Anaheim, California, to 96-2-1 Mexican legend Julio Cesar Chavez, the future Hall of Famer and six-time, three-division world champion. Chavez was coming off his disappointing TKO loss to Oscar de la Hoya when he fought Gamache, who was penalized a point for headbutting in the fifth round. Cut over the right eyebrow, Gamache retired after the eighth round in a harder fight than most expected against the Mexican superstar. The October 12, 1996 card also featured stars such as Erik Morales, Michael Carbajal, Joe Luis Castillo, and Daniel Santos.

Gamache won his next nine fights, mostly against journeyman, to earn him a shot at ultra-popular Arturo Gatti (30-4), the future Hall of Famer and former WBC light welterweight world champion, on February 26, 2000, in Madison Square Garden. This fight would disappointedly mark the end of Gamache's career, because he became the center of controversy after the official weigh in and subsequently its damaging results in the ring.

A New York State Athletic Commission (NYSAC) official allowed Gatti to step off the scale before it was determined if Gatti had made the contracted 141-pound weight limit. Team Gamache's protests were ignored and, according to HBO, Gatti reportedly entered the ring weighing 160 pounds, nineteen more than Gamache. The larger Gatti brutally defeated a gutsy Gamache, ending things in the second round with a knockout that caused brain damage for Gamache, who was hospitalized for days and ultimately forced into retirement due to his severe injury.

Gamache filed a lawsuit against the NYSAC, alleging Gatti weighed considerably more than the contracted weight. Judge Melvin Schweitzer ruled in Gamache's favor due to the NYSAC improperly conducting the weigh in. However, Judge Schweitzer was not convinced that the NYSA's weigh-in negligence was not the substantial factor in the injury. Even though he wasn't awarded financial damages, Gamache considered the verdict a victory, because it upheld his good name and integrity.

"For a while it did bother me," Gamache spoke about his final fight. "It was a tough loss fighting that way. I was 33 at that time. No fighter wants to go out that way with a knockout loss, but it happens to some of the best."

Unable to continue boxing, Gamache was recruited by legendary trainer Emanuel Steward to become an assistant trainer at the famed Kronk Gym. Joey has worked with the Klitschko brothers Wladimir and Vitali, Vasyl Lomachenko, and Teófimo Lopez, among world champions, and more recently he's served as the head trainer for heavyweight Otto Wallin.

"Training with Emmanuel Stewart in Detroit for a while was a great experience. I learned boxing from him. He was a great man and trainer."

What did becoming world champion mean to him?

"Meant everything to me," Gamache quickly answered. "I'd always dreamed it. People were always good to me back home. I had a good fanbase. They rooted for me. I had a lot of support and that meant a lot. Not everybody lives a dream like I did. I was fortunate and, again, it took a good team."

Joey Gamache is the one and only world boxing champion from Maine. All four of his pro losses were to world champions, but unfortunately he's best remembered by some for the tragic results of his last fight instead of his tremendous accomplishments.

ALL-NEW ENGLAND

Birth Name:	Joseph Gamache
Born:	May 20, 1966, in Bath, Maine
Hometown:	Lewiston, Maine
Amateurs:	84-12, 1982 National Junior Olympics, 1984 National Golden Gloves silver medalist
Pro Record:	55-4 (38 KOs, 4 KOBY)
Pro Titles:	WBA world super featherweight champion (June 28, 1991– vacated 1991), WBA lightweight world champion (June 13, 1992–October 24, 1992)
Pro Career:	1987–2000
Height:	5' 6"
Reach:	64"
Stance:	Orthodox
Division:	Super lightweight, lightweight, and super featherweight

World Title Fight Record: 2-2 (2 KOs, 2 KOBY)
Records vs. World Champions: 0-4, 4 KOBY), lost to Tony Lopez, Julio Cesar Chavez,*
Orzubek Nazarov, Arturo Gatti* (* International Boxing HOF)

Trainer:	Tony Lampron, Teddy Atlas, Jimmy Glenn

Notes: Gamache won the International Boxing Federation (IBF) Inter-Continental super featherweight title in 1990 via a fourth-round TKO of Irving Mitchell in Lewiston. Gamache successfully defended his IBF Inter-Continental super featherweight crown against Nelson Rodriguez and Jeff Franklin.

No. 25

MICKY WARD

"Irish"
A Real Fighter's Fighter

Numerous broken bones and ear drums, countless stitches and concussions, multiple operations, and his classic balls-to-the-wall style ingratiated "Irish" Micky Ward to boxing fans and into boxing folklore. Of course, highlighted by his epic trilogy of fights with his rival and eventual close friend Arturo Gatti.

Always prepared to give his absolute best without ever trashing his opponent, Ward developed a passionate fan base that continues to grow today, largely because of the incredible respect they have for one of boxing's most beloved ring warriors, who in four years went from earning $500 per fight during his comeback to becoming the first fighter with double digit losses (eleven) to earn a cool $1 million in his second clash with Gatti.

Many of Ward's friends and relatives, especially his brother Dicky Eklund (who later became his head trainer), turned Micky on to boxing at an early age. Lowell, Massachusetts, has been the amateur boxing epicenter for the past seventy-five-plus years. New England's Central Golden Gloves Tournament is annually held there, as well as the New England Tournament of Champions (open and novice finals of the New England Golden Gloves competition).

Ward's first boxing match was at the age of seven, when he was matched against Joey Roach, the brother of Hall of Fame trainer Freddie Roach. He doesn't remember the final result, but it signaled the start of his boxing career, as well as igniting the fire in his stomach that burned brightly. He retired from the ring in 2003. The memories he left behind are still repeatedly watched—particularly the inspiring Gatti-Ward trilogy—by old and new boxing fans who live to watch a good fight. Ward gave everything he had in each fight, whether he won or lost. That's the way he was made.

"Growing up in New England was good and obviously the Golden Gloves in my hometown (Lowell) was huge," Ward remembered when it all started for him. "The Nationals (Golden Gloves Tournament) was held there a few times. Lowell is a boxing town for amateurs, but pro boxing isn't really big in Lowell. New England isn't a hotbed for pro boxing like Philadelphia, New York, Los Angeles, Detroit, Chicago, or other places. World champions from New England have been few and far between. I had to go to Atlantic City to get big fights. I fought there twenty something times.

"I only went outside of New England once for a training camp. We went to Miami for sparring and (Ward's co-trainer for one fight vs. Jesse James Leija) Pat Byrne had a US National amateur champion, Lamar Murphy. Some fighters left New England for training camp for better weather and sparring, but we brought in guys for big fights. Another reason to go outside of New England to train was to get away from temptations. I didn't have to leave home to train because I was focused on winning, and I was more comfortable at home."

His eighteen-year professional boxing career officially began on June 13, 1985, at a nearby rink, Roll-On-America Skating Rink, in Lawrence, Massachusetts. He returned two months later, fighting at home in the venue that he first made his name in, Lowell Memorial Auditorium, stopping Greg Young in the second round. He found a second home, Atlantic City, New Jersey, where he fought his next seven fights—including four at future United States President Donald J. Trump's casino (Trump Casino Hotel)—before returning home to Lowell with a 9-0 (7 KOs) record to face intra-state rival John Rafuse

(12-2) of Malden. Ward took an eight-round unanimous decision and soon extended his record to 12-0 when he made his Las Vegas debut outdoors at the famed Caesars Palace, fighting on a card headlined by the world middleweight title fight between "Sugar" Ray Leonard and Marvelous Marvin Hagler, stopping Kelly Kobie in the fourth round.

Ward's undefeated streak ended at 14-0, when another Massachusetts fighter, 21-7-2 Puerto Rico native and Chelsea resident Edwin Curet, won a ten-round split decision in Atlantic City. Micky became an Atlantic City regular, but he started being thrown in with larger, more experienced fighters such as 17-2 Mike Mungin, who outweighed Ward by eight and a half pounds at the weigh in and considerably more in the ring. Mungin won a close ten-round unanimous decision (95-94, 95-94, 96-93) in spite of their critical weight differential.

Three months later, also in Atlantic City, Micky bounced back strong with a 3rd-round technical knockout of 30-3 Francisco Tomas da Cruz, earning him a high exposure fight with 28-1 Frankie Warren, who kept his USBA by way of a ten-round unanimous decision in Atlantic City. Back to back wins versus 13-3-1 Clarence Coleman and 14-1 David Rivello, respectively by fifth-round TKO and ten-round split decision, led to Ward's four-fight losing streak. In order, against 67-10-1 Harold Brazier (LDEC12) for the IBF Inter-Continental super lightweight title; 17-0 and future world champion Charles Murray (LDEC12) in his Rochester, New York, hometown for the USBA championship; 22-3 Tony Martin (LDEC10); and 15-1 Ricky Myers (LDEC10). The three non-Murray fights were all held in Atlantic City.

Tired of losing and the politics of boxing, Ward was burned out, so he chose to take the next three years off. Micky returned to the ring on June 17, 1994, but on his terms and, of course, at home in Lowell against journeyman Luis Castillo, who was knocked out in round five. He had three more tune-ups and was ready to take on undefeated Louis Veader (31-0), an up and coming fighter from Rhode Island, at TD Garden (which replaced the old Boston Garden and home of the Boston Celtics and Boston Bruins) for the WBU intercontinental light welterweight title. Ward scored a ninth-round knockout, and three months later he successfully defended his strap, winning a twelve-round unanimous decision at Foxwoods Resort Casino, followed by a ten-round split decision over 13-6-2 Manny Castillo.

Riding a nine-fight win streak, Ward was matched against undefeated rising star Alfonso Sanchez (16-0) at Thomas & Mack Center in Las Vegas, in the cofeature on the Oscar de la Hoya-Pernell Whitaker card. Ward turned in arguably the worst performance of his life, losing every second of each round, bashed by HBO broadcasters for his disappointing fight; that is, until the seventh round, when Mickey's notorious left hook to the liver paralyzed Sanchez. His knockout of Sanchez set the stage for Ward's first and only major world title fight four months later against IBF super lightweight world champion Vince Phillips (36-3) at The Roxy in downtown Boston. Phillips took the first two rounds, and a bad cut over Ward's eye resulted in the ring physician ending the fight.

Ward's ring return was eight months later, when he stopped 33-17-1 Mark Fernandez at Foxwoods. Up next was an Interim USBA super lightweight fight versus Zab Judah (15-0), the future six-time, two-division world champion. The speedy Judah was too quick and fast for Ward to catch with any consistency, but to this day Judah claims that Ward was the toughest fighter he ever faced, and that at one point he wanted to quit after getting a taste of Ward's body attack.

Micky had fought with one hand for too long, suffering a break that he couldn't afford to repair, although that's what led to his trademark left hook to the body that crippled many of his opponents. After being sidelined for eight months, he returned to action on March 17, 1999, with two good hands, knocking out Jose Luis Mendez in the third round at The Roxy. Ward had become a regular on ESPN, and the real magic began on October 1, 1999, against 30-3 Reggie Green at the Hampton Casino in New Hampshire. Green led going into the tenth and final round and Ward kept up his relentless attack, finally finishing off Green at the 2:40 mark. A spent Ward was literally carried into his locker-room before his customary trip to the hospital. Looking back now, without his dramatic comeback and ending, the legend of Micky Ward wouldn't have happened.

Ward accepted a fight in England to face undefeated WBU world super lightweight titlist Shea Neary (22-0), a popular Irishman who was on the fast track to stardom. A raucous crowd, including celebrities such as rocker Mick Jagger, enjoyed the first few rounds against the normally slow starting Ward, who nevertheless kept coming on with intense pressure, finally catching Neary and sending him across the ring like a rag doll. Ward's damaging punches led referee Mickey Vann to wave off the fight in the eighth round.

The WBU title was considered a European belt, and Ward didn't receive his belt until four months later after threatening a lawsuit, only to lose it in his next fight, even though the title wasn't on the line. An obscure WBU rule was that its champions would lose their title belt off a losing effort even if it were a non-title fight. Invader Antonio Diaz (34-2) narrowly pulled out a victory at Foxwoods, taking a ten-round unanimous decision.

In his first 2001 fight, Ward destroyed 26-8 veteran Steve Quiñonez with a patented left hook to the body in the opening round at Foxwoods that immobilized Quiñonez, who was unaware that he had broken Micky's eardrum. Years later, the mere mention of Ward's name in a phone conversation I had with Steve at once led to a grunting response as he said he could still feel the pain from the aforementioned body shot.

By now a fixture on ESPN, Ward's final appearance on the worldwide network turned out to be in the 2001 Fight of the Year, in which he went toe to toe against Emanuel Augustus at the Hampton Casino in Hampton, New Hampshire. Ward dropped the always tough Augustus on his way to an entertaining win by ten-round unanimous decision in a fight much closer than the final judges' scores indicated (98-90, 96-91, 96-94). Ward believes that his was one of his best fights against one of his toughest opponents.

HBO was interested in matching Ward against Gatti, who was a human highlight film in the ring, and gave Micky a "tryout" against 42-5-2 Jesse James Leija in his San Antonio backyard. Ward came out firing and busted up Leija's face, opening up a large cut over his eye. Referee Laurence Cole, however, called the cut was from a headbutt because, "I didn't see a punch and assumed it was a head butt." Leija lasted the required four rounds to make the fight official and suddenly he was unable to continue in the fifth. The Texan won a five-round technical split decision by scores of 49-46, 48-47 and 47-48. Team Ward later protested but it went nowhere with Texas boxing head Dickie Cole, the father of the referee. The mood in the locker room after the fight was gloomy because everybody felt that the loss eliminated Ward from his first major money fight against Gatti. Ward's promoter, Lou DiBella, caught up with the limousine transporting Team Ward back to the hotel, jumped inside, and yelled loudly that HBO understood that Ward had been ripped off. HBO continually aired a replay of the punch in question over and over during the broadcast, and the slow-motion version clearly showed it was a punch, not a headbutt that caused Leija's cut.

The 2002 Fight of the Year happened on May 18, 2002, at Mohegan Sun Arena. Tens of thousands have since claimed that they were in attendance, but the 10,000-seat arena really only had around 6,500 fans there, and hundreds of thousands watched on HBO. What they saw was memorable, especially the 2002 Round of the Year (ninth), when it looked like Leija was done. Somehow, in typical Gatti fashion, he survived, and the two combatants put on a show for the ages, with Ward winning a ten-round majority decision (94-93, 95-93, 94-94).

The rematch was held six months later at Gatti's house, Boardwalk Hotel in Atlantic City, and Micky signed for a $1 million payday—a first for a fighter with double-digit losses. Ward got caught early, sending his equilibrium into a deliberating state, and he never really recovered in a fairly one-sided loss on points.

The trilogy was completed in the 2003 Fight of the Year, also held at Boardwalk Hall and aired live on HBO like the previous two clashes. The action went back and forth, not nearly as quite as intense as their original fight, but it certainly was memorable.

Ward had announced prior to Gatti-Ward III that it would be his last even if he were offered another $1 million payday, which he was, but he stayed true to his word, remaining retired, never to fight again.

As much as fans all around the world remember the blood and guts action, they won't forget how the two fighters became as close as brothers, laughing and joking in the hospital, hugging and kissing each other's cheeks prior to the final rounds, praising each other endlessly out of their mutual respect and admiration. Ward even trained Gatti for one of his last fights.

"My first fight with Arturo Gatti was my best fight and it was held in New England at Mohegan Sun," Ward noted. "I was in two Ring magazine's Fight of the Year there (Mohegan Sun in Uncasville, CT) and in New Hampshire (Hampton Beach). I don't think that ever happened before (2 FOY in NE). I still don't realize what I've done. I guess I'm just humble. I'm glad it happened and I'm proud of it. I can say I did it, but I'd rather be known as a good, all-around person. Me and Arturo had respect for each other from our first fight and it grew into us becoming close friends. What I respected most about him was shown on HBO, when I was lying in a hospital bed and my doctor (Dr. Steve Margles) pulled back the curtain and Arturo was lying there in the next bed; the first thing he said was, 'Mick, are you OK?' That was the first thing he said to me after we tried to kill each other for 30 rounds."

The Gatti-Ward Trilogy propelled Micky into celebrity status, from attending the 2011 Academy Awards with fellow Bay Stater Mark Wahlberg, who played Micky in the highly acclaimed movie *The Fighter* released in 2010. (Wahlberg is reportedly negotiating for a sequel that would be about the Gatti-Ward trilogy.) Ward has had a pair of books (*Irish Thunder: The Hard Life, Times of Micky Ward* by Bob Halloran and his biography *The Warriors Heart: The True Story of Life Before and Beyond The Fighter*, written with Joe Layden) written about him, along with two songs ("The Warriors Code" by Dropkick Murphys and "Animal Rap," known as the "Micky Ward Mix") by Jedi Mind Tricks, and video game Fight Night Round 3, featuring Ward and Gatti on the cover. Not too shabby for a guy who completed his pro career with a 38-13 (27 KOs) record but with a lifetime of incredible action fights.

Boxers such as Micky Ward always brought much more than his shorts, gloves, and mouthpiece into the ring. Wins, losses, and titles always mean something in the not so always "Sweet Science," but his intrinsic values, working-class attitude, and dogged determination made this popular Irish American boxer very special to his legion of fans from all around the world, as well as those throughout the industry itself. His legacy will last as long as boxing still is a sport.

The humble, unassuming Ward, though, will be just as happily remembered, as he calls it, as an honest fighter. What he is, though, and will always remain, is a fighter's fighter.

ALL-NEW ENGLAND

Birth Name:	George Michael Ward Jr.
Nickname:	Irish
Born:	October 4, 1965, in Lowell, Massachusetts
Hometown:	Lowell, Massachusetts
Amateurs:	62-10, three-time New England Golden Gloves champion
Pro Record:	38-13 (27 KOs, 1 KOBY)
Pro Career:	1985–2003
Height:	5' 8"
Reach:	70"
Stance:	Orthodox
Division:	Super lightweight

World Title Fight Record: 0-1 (1 KOBY)
Records vs. World Champions: 1-6 (0 KO, 1 KOBY), Arturo Gatti*; lost to Arturo Gatti (2),* Jesse James Leija, Zab Judah, Vince Phillips, Charles Murray

Managers:	Alice Ward, Sal Lonano
Trainers:	Dicky Eklund, Mickey O'Keefe, Pat Burns

Notes: Three-time Fight of the Year participant: 2001 vs. Emanuel Augustus, 2002 Arturo Gatti I, and 2003 Arturo Gatti III—it marked the first time a fighter had been in three consecutive Fights of the Year since the sixties with Rocky Marciano and Carmen Basilio; only time he was stopped was in 1997 vs. Vince Phillips for the IBF world title in the third round of their Boston fight on cuts; boxed in the same weight class, junior welterweight/super lightweight, his entire pro career; strengthened his upper body through his road paving job; world champions Gatti and Zab Judah said Ward was the toughest opponent they ever fought

HONORABLE MENTIONS
(listed alphabetically)

SAL BARTOLO

Born: November 11, 1917, in Boston, MA; **Hometown:** East Boston, MA; **Died:** February 19, 2002; **Pro Record:** 73-18-6 (16 KOs, 2 KOBY); **Pro Career:** 1937–1949; **Division:** featherweight

If not for Willie Pep, who Bartolo lost to three times, Sal Bartolo would likely be in the top twenty-five. His second fight and loss by fifteen-round unanimous decision to defending champion Pep at Braves Field in Boston was for the New York State Athletic Commission World Featherweight Championship

Bartolo was a New England champion when it really meant something. In 1944, "The Pride of East Boston" defeated defending National Boxing Association (NBA) World Featherweight champion Phil Terranova. Bartolo's snapping jab, damaging hooks, and superior footwork led to Bartolo's near fifteen-round shutout at a packed Boston Garden. Two fights later, Bartolo successfully defended his NBA crown at the Boston Garden, taking a fifteen-round split decision. In 1946, Bartolo knocked out Spider Armstrong, again at The Garden, in his second title defense, but he later lost again to NBA champion Pep by way of a twelfth round knockout at Madison Square Garden.

MELIO BETTINA

Born: November 18, 1916, in Beacon, NY; **Hometown:** Bridgeport, CT; **Died:** December 20, 1996; **Pro Record:** 83-14-3 (36 KOs, 3 KOBY); **Pro Career:** 1934–1948; **Division:** heavyweight and light heavyweight

In 1939, Melio Bettina captured the vacant New York State Athletic Commission World Light Heavyweight title by upsetting Tiger Jack Fox (99-15-10) via a ninth-round technical knockout. This TKO set the stage for a July 13, 1939, challenge by popular Billy Conn (46-9-1) before 15,295 fans at the famed Madison Square Garden in New York City. Conn won a fifteen-round unanimous decision (10-5, 8-7, 9-6) and the title. Three months later, future HOF inductee Conn successfully defended his belt versus Bettina, winning another fifteen-round unanimous decision.

Bettina won, lost, and fought to a draw in his trilogy with Hall of Famer Jimmy Bivins, in addition to splitting a pair of 1940 fights against another Hall of Famer, Fred Apostoli.

PADDY DUFFY

Born: November 12, 1864, in Boston, MA; **Hometown:** Boston, MA; **Died:** July 19, 1890; **Pro Record:** 31-3-16 (18 KOs, 1 KOBY); **Pro Career:** 1884-1889; **Division:** welterweight; IBHOF: Class of 2008.

Paddy Duffy captured the first World Welterweight Championship on March 29, 1889, in San Francisco, when he defeated Tom Meadows in the 45th round by disqualification. Duffy never defended his title belt, because he became sick and died from tuberculosis at the age of 25, merely 15 months after he was crowned.

MIKE GLOVER

Born: December 18, 1890, in Lawrence, MA; **Hometown:** Lawrence, MA; **Died:** July 11, 1917; **Pro Record:** 30-5-5 (16 KOs, 1 KOBY): **Pro Career:** 1908–1916; **Division:** welterweight

Born Michael Cavanaugh, Mike Glover died thirteen months after his last pro fight, a twelve-round loss by points to Hall of Famer Ted "Kid" Lewis at the Boston Arena. He faced Lewis, a Brit who lived for several years in Chelsea, Massachusetts, winning and losing twelve-round decisions on points. Glover also fought two draws with Hall of Famer Battling Levinsky.

Glover became the world welterweight champion in 1915, when he won a twelve-round decision over Matt Wells at the Boston Arena. Unfortunately (at least for Glover), he then became the most dubious world champion with the shortest reign, only twenty-one days, when Hall of Famer Jack Britton won a twelve-round decision at the Boston Arena. Glover split two other matches with Britton, both by decision.

HAROLD GOMES

Born: August 22, 1933, in Providence, RI; **Hometown:** Providence, RI: **Pro Record:** 52-10 (24 KOs, 7 KOBY); **Pro Career:** 1951–1963; **Division:** lightweight, super featherweight, and featherweight

An underrated fighter who was a New England featherweight champion, Harold Gomes became world super featherweight champion in 1959, when he overcame four knockdowns to win a fifteen-round unanimous decision in East Providence, Rhode Island.

Gomes' main problem was being in the same division as Filipino star and future Hall of Famer Flash Elorde, who in 1960 stopped Gomes in round seven of his first title defense in the Philippines. Five months later, in a rematch, Elorde knocked out Gomes in the opening round in California.

JAKE KILRIAN

Born: February 9, 1889, Greenpoint, NY; **Hometown:** Quincy, MA; **Died:** December 22, 1937; **Pro Record:** 31-5-8 (18 KOs, 4 KOBY); **Pro Career:** 1879–1899; **Division:** heavyweight

Born Jack Kilrain, he changed his name to Jake to hide his fighting from his parents. A celebrated rower who used that training to strengthen his power, Kilrain was inducted in the Bare Knuckle and International Boxing halls of fame.

In bare knuckle, Kilrain was the United States national champion, who trolled John L. Sullivan to fight due to Sullivan allegedly disrespecting Kilrain, especially after Jake defeated Brit favorite Jem Smith in 106 rounds to be called world champion, which was the title Sullivan claimed to hold. The two finally fought in 1887 under unhealthy conditions (104 degrees) in Richburg, Mississippi. After fighting two hours, sixteen minutes, Kilrain's chief second admitted defeat during the seventy-sixth round because his charge's eyes were practically closed and he was bleeding profusely from the nose and lips. Sullivan vs. Kilrain was the last World Bare Knuckle Championship match.

Kilrain was also a standout boxer who defeated George Godfrey (who fought out of Revere, Massachusetts) in two of three fights with a draw, as well as William Sheriff. Kilrain fought a draw with Charlie Mitchell and lost to James J. Corbett.

HONEY MELLODY

Born: January 15, 1984, in Charlestown, MA; **Hometown:** Charlestown, MA; **Died:** March 2, 1991; **Pro Record:** 48-17-21 (30 KOs, 6 KOBY); **Pro Career:** 1902–1913; **Division:** welterweight

William "Honey" Mellody claimed the world "white" 142-pound title in 1904 by decisioning Matty Mathews in twelve rounds, world "white" 145-pound championship by knocking out Martin Duffy in the fourth round, and lost the strap to Buddy Ryan when he was stopped in the first round.

Mellody won the World Welterweight Championship in 1906, taking a fifteen-round decision on points versus Joe Walcott in Chelsea, Massachusetts, and a month and a half later he knocked out Walcott in the twelfth round of his first title defense in Chelsea. In 1907, Mellody successfully defended his crown against Terry Martin by way of a fifteen-round decision. Later that year, Mellody lost his crown when he was knocked out in the fifteenth round by Frank Mantell. Melody's final world title fight came in 1908, in which he was knocked out in the fourth round by Harry Lewis.

RAY "Sucra" OLIVEIRA

Born: October 6, 1968, in New Bedford, MA; **Hometown:** New Bedford, MA; **Pro Record:** 47-11-2 (22 KOs, 2 KOBY); **Pro Career:** 1990–2005; **Division:** super lightweight

An all-action fighter with tremendous defensive skills, Ray Oliveira never held a world title, but he defeated three world champions: Charles Murray (twice), Vince Phillips, and Vivian Harris.

A two-time NABF champion, Oliveira and Phillips combined for a record 463 punches thrown in a single round, and the 2,729 combined thrown punches in a loss by twelve-round decision to Ben Tackie ranks third-most in boxing history.

CHICO "Stamford's Socking Schoolboy" VEJAR

Born: September 5, 1931in Stamford, CT; **Hometown:** Stamford, CT; **Died:** September 19, 2016; **Pro Record:** 92-20-4 (43 KOs, 3 KOBY), **Pro Career:** 1950–1961; **Division:** welterweight

Francis Vejar, who became a movie actor after he retired from the ring, never fought for a world title. The closest he came was in a 1955 world title eliminator, when he was knocked out in the opening round by future Hall of Famer and world champion Tony Demarco.

Vejar fought the best of his era, losing to Hall of Famers Joey Giardello (twice), Gene Fullmer, and Kid Gavilan. Vejar did score two wins by decision over Hall of Famer Billy Graham twice.

RALPH "The Ripper" ZANELLI

Born: October 2, 1915, in Seneca Falls, NY; **Hometown:** Providence, RI; **Died:** November 29, 2006; **Pro Record:** 93-49-7 (33 KOs, 4 KOBY); **Pro Career:** 1936-1952;; **Division**: middleweight and welterweight

Ralph Zanelli was a true anybody, anytime, anyplace type of fighter. He was the 1936 New England Golden Gloves champion as an amateur, and went on to become a New England welterweight and middleweight champion as a professional. In his only world title fight, he was knocked out by Hall of Famer Henry Armstrong in the fifth round at the Boston Garden.

Zanelli upset Hall of Famer Fritzie Zivic in 1943 at the Boston Garden, taking a ten-round decision for his statement victory. The tough-as-nails Zanelli also took the following Hall of Famers the full distance: Armstrong (twice), Sugar Ray Robinson, Sammy Angott, Kid Gavilan, and Ike Williams. In 1987, Zanelli was inducted into the Rhode Island Heritage Hall of Fame, and a year later he went into the Italian American Sports Hall of Fame.

WORLD CHAMPIONSHIP FIGHTS BY TOP NEW ENGLAND FIGHTERS

Willie Pep

Sept. 8, 1959   Sandy Saddler (115-7-2)   LRTD8   New York, New York, USA
    (World Featherweight Championship)

Mar. 17, 1950   Ray Famechon (59-5)   WDEC15   New York, New York, USA
    (World Featherweight Championship)

Jan. 16, 1950   Charley Riley (51-11-2)   WKO5   St. Louis, Missouri, USA
    (World Featherweight Championship)

Sept. 20, 1949   Eddie Compo (57-1-3)   WTKO7   **Waterbury, Connecticut**, USA
    (World Featherweight Championship)

Feb. 11, 1949   Sandy Saddler (92-6-2)   WDEC15   New York, New York, USA
    (World Featherweight Championship)

Oct. 29, 1948   Sandy Saddler (86-6-2)   LKO4   New York, New York, USA
    (World Featherweight Championship)

Feb. 24, 1948   Humberto Sierra (40-7-3)   WTKO10   Miami, Florida, USA
    (World Featherweight Championship)

Aug. 22, 1947   Jock Leslie (58-9-4)   WKO12   Flint, Michigan, ISA
    (World Featherweight Championship)

June 7, 1946   Sal Bartolo (71-17-6)   WKO12   New York, New York, USA
    (NBA and NYSAC World Featherweight Championship)

Feb. 19, 1945   Phil Terranova (36-11-9)   WDEC15   New York, New York, USA
    (NYSAC World Featherweight Championship)

Sept. 29, 1944   Chalky Wright (162-34-18)   WDEC15   New York, New York, USA
    (NYSAC World Featherweight Championship)

June 8, 1943   Sal Bartolo (45-15-6)   WDEC15   **Boston, Massachusetts**, USA
                (NYSAC World Featherweight Championship)
Nov. 20, 1942   Chalky Wright (143-32-17) WDEC15   New York, New York, USA
                (NYSAC World Featherweight Championship)

Rocky Marciano

Sept. 21, 1955   Archie Moore (149-19-8)   WKO9   Bronx, New York, USA
                (NBA World Heavyweight Championship)
May 16, 1955   Don Cockell (66-11-1)   WTKO9   San Francisco, California, USA
                (NBA World Featherweight Championship)
Sept. 17, 1954   Ezzard Charles (85-11-1)   WKO8   Bronx, New York, USA
                (NBA World Featherweight Championship)
June 17, 1954   Ezzard Charles (85-10-1)   WDEC15   Bronx, New York, USA
                (NBA World Featherweight Championship)
Sept. 24, 1953   Roland LaStarza (53-3-1)   WTKO11   New York, New York, USA
                (NBA World Featherweight Championship)
May 15, 1953   Jersey Joe Walcott (49-19-1) WKO1   Chicago, Illinois, USA
                (NBA World Featherweight Championship)
Sept. 23, 1952   Jersey Joe Walcott (49-18-1) WKO13   Philadelphia, Pennsylvania, USA
                (NBA World Featherweight Championship)

Marvin Hagler

Apr. 6, 1987   Ray Leonard (33-1)   LDEC12   Las Vegas, Nevada, USA
                (WBC World Middleweight Championship)
Mar. 10, 1986   John Mugabi (25-0)   WKO11   Las Vegas, Nevada, USA
                (WBC, WBA, and IBF World Middleweight Championships)
Apr. 15, 1985   Thomas Hearns (40-1)   WTKO3   Las Vegas, Nevada, USA
                (WBC, WBA, and IBF World Middleweight Championships)
Oct. 19, 1984   Mustafa Hamsho (38-2-2)   WTKO3   Las Vegas, Nevada, USA
                (WBC and WBA World Middleweight Championships)
Mar. 30, 1984   Juan Domingo Roldán (52-2-2) WTKO10   Las Vegas, Nevada, USA
                (WBC, WBA, and IBF World Middleweight Championships)
Nov. 10, 1983   Roberto Duran (77-4)   WDEC15   Las Vegas, Nevada, USA

(WBC, WBA, and IBF World Middleweight Championships)

| May 27, 1983 | Wilford Scypion (26-3) | WKO4 | **Providence, Rhode Island**, USA |

(IBF World Middleweight Championship)

| Feb. 11, 1983 | Tony Sibson (47-3-1) | WTKO6 | **Worcester, Massachusetts**, USA |

(WBC and WBA World Middleweight Championships)

| Oct. 30, 1982 | Fulgencio Obelmejias (38-1) | WTKO5 | San Remo, Liguria, Italy |

(WBC and WBA World Middleweight Championships)

| Mar. 7, 1982 | Caveman Lee (21-2) | WTKO1 | Atlantic City, New Jersey, USA |

(WBC and WBA World Middleweight Championships)

| Oct. 3, 1981 | Mustafa Hamsho (32-1-2) | WTKO11 | Rosemont, Illinois, USA |

(WBC and WBA World Middleweight Championships)

| June 13, 1981 | Vito Antuofermo (46-5-2) | WRTD4 | **Boston, Massachusetts**, USA |

(WBC and WBA World Middleweight Championships)

| Sept. 27, 1980 | Alan Minter (38-6) | WTKO3 | Wembley, London, UK |

(WBC and WBA World Middleweight Championships)

| Nov. 30, 1979 | Vito Antuofermo (45-3-1) | D15 | Las Vegas, Nevada, USA |

(WBC and WBA World Middleweight Championships)

Sam Langford

| Sept. 5, 1904 | Joe Walcott (87-15-17) | D15 | **Manchester, New Hampshire**, USA |

(World Welterweight Championship)

John L. Sullivan

| Aug. 29, 1885 | Dominick McCaffrey (7-2-3) | WDEC7 | Cincinnati, Ohio, USA |

(Inaugural World Heavyweight Championship)

Vinny Pazienza

Mar. 1, 2002   Eric Lucas (34-4-3)   LDEC12   **Mashantucket, Connecticut**, USA
(WBC World Middleweight Championship)

June 24, 1995   Roy Jones, Jr. (28-0)   LTKO6   Atlantic City, New Jersey, USA
(IBF World Super Middleweight Championship)

Oct. 1, 1991   Gilbert Dele (29-0-1)   WTKO12   **Providence, Rhode Island**, USA
(WBA World Super Middleweight Championship)

Dec. 1, 1990   Loreto Garza (27-1-1)   LDQ11   Sacramento, California, USA
(WBA World Super Lightweight Championship)

Feb. 3, 1990   Hector Camacho (36-0)   LDEC12   Atlantic City, New Jersey, USA
(WBO World Super Lightweight Championship)

Nov. 7, 1988   Rober Mayweather (33-5)   LDEC12   Las Vegas, Nevada, USA
(WBC Super Lightweight Championship)

Feb. 6, 1988   Greg Haugen (20-1)   LDEC15   Atlantic City, New Jersey, USA
(IBF World Lightweight Championship)

June 7, 1987   Greg Haugen (19-0)   WDEC15   **Providence, Rhode Island**, USA
(IBF World Lightweight Championship)

Tony DeMarco

Nov. 30, 1955   Carmen Basilio (47-11-7)   LTKO12   **Boston, Massachusetts**, USA
(World Welterweight Championship)

June 10, 1955   Carmen Basilio (44-11-7)   LTKO12   Syracuse, New York, USA
(World Welterweight Championship)

Apr. 1, 1955   Johnny Saxton (46-3-2)   WTKO14   **Boston, Massachusetts**, USA
(World Welterweight Championship)

Jack Sharkey

June 29, 1933   Primo Carnera (75-6)   LKO6   New York, New York, USA
(NBA World and NYSAC World Heavyweight Championship)

June 21, 1932   Max Schmeling (44-4-3)   WDEC15   Queens, New York, USA

	(NYSAC World Heavyweight Championship)		
June 12, 1930	Max Schmeling (42-4-3) LDQ4		Bronx, New York, USA
	(vacant NBA World and NYSAC World Championships)		

Paul Pender

Apr. 7, 1962	Terry Downes (28-7)	WDEC15	**Boston, Massachusetts**, USA
	(World Middleweight Championship)		
July 11, 1961	Terry Downes (27-7)	LRTD9	Wembley, London, UK
	(World Middleweight Championship)		
Apr. 22, 1961	Carmen Basilio (56-15-7)	WDEC15	**Boston, Massachusetts**, USA
	(World Middleweight Championship)		
Jan. 14, 1961	Terry Downes (25-6)	WTKO7	**Boston, Massachusetts**, USA
	(World Middleweight Championship)		
June 10, 1960	Ray Robinson (144-7-2)	WDEC15	**Boston, Massachusetts**, USA
	(World Middleweight Championship)		
Jan. 22, 1960	Ray Robinson (143-6-2)	WDEC15	**Boston, Massachusetts**, USA
	(World Middleweight Championship)		

Marlon Starling

Aug. 19, 1990	Maurice Blocker (31-1)	LDEC12	Reno, Nevada, USA
	(WBC World Welterweight Championship)		
Apr. 14, 1990	Michael Nunn (34-0)	LDEC12	Las Vegas, Nevada, USA
	(IBF World Middleweight Championship)		
Sept. 15, 1989	Young Kil Jong (27-4-2)	WDEC12	**Hartford, Connecticut**, USA
	(WBC World Welterweight Championship)		
Feb. 4, 1989	Lloyd Honeyghan (33-1)	WTKO9	Las Vegas, Nevada, USA
	(WBC World Welterweight Championship)		
Apr. 16, 1988	Mark Breland (20-1)	D12	Las Vegas, Nevada, USA
	(WBA World Welterweight Championship)		
Feb. 5, 1988	Fujio Ozaki (21-4)	WDEC12	Atlantic City, New Jersey, USA
	(WBA World Welterweight Championship)		
Aug. 22, 1987	Mark Breland (18-0)	WTKO11	Columbia, South Carolina, USA
	(WBA World Welterweight Championship)		

Feb. 4, 1984   Donald Curry (17-0)   LDEC15   Atlantic City, New Jersey, USA
               (WBA World and IBF World Welterweight Championships)

Chad Dawson

June 8, 2013   Adonis Stevenson (20-1)   LKO1   Montreal, Quebec, Canada
               (WBC World Light Heavyweight Championship)
Sept. 8, 2012   Andre Ward (25-0)   LTKO10   Oakland, California, USA
               (WBC World and WBA World Light Heavyweight Championships)
April 28, 2012   Bernard Hopkins (52-5-2)   WDEC12   Atlantic City, New Jersey, USA
               (WBC World Light Heavyweight Championship)
Aug. 14, 2010   Jean Pascal (25-1)   LTD1   Montreal, Quebec, Canada
               (WBC World Light Heavyweight Championship)
Nov. 7, 2009   Glen Johnson (49-12-2)   WDEC12   **Hartford, Connecticut**, USA
               (WBC World Interim Light Heavyweight Championship)
May 9, 2009   Antonio Tarver (27-5)   WDEC12   Las Vegas, Nevada, USA
               (IBF World Light Heavyweight Championship)
Oct. 11, 2008   Antonio Tarver (27-4)   WDEC12   Las Vegas, Nevada, USA
               (IBF World Light Heavyweight Championship)
Apr. 12, 2008   Glen Johnson (47-11-2)   WDEC12   Tampa, Florida, USA
               (WBC World Light Heavyweight Championship)
Sept. 29, 2007   Epifanio Mendoza (28-4-1)   WTKO4   Sacramento, California, USA
               (WBC World Light Heavyweight Championship)
June 9, 2007   Jesus Ruiz (19-4)   WTKO6   **Hartford, Connecticut**, USA
               (WBC World Light Heavyweight Championship)
Feb. 3, 2007   Tomasz Adamek (31-0)   WDEC12   Kissimmee, Florida, USA

Louis Kaplan

June 28, 1926   Bobby Garcia (53-25-7)   WTKO10   **Hartford, Connecticut**, USA
               (World Featherweight Championship)
Dec. 18, 1925   Babe Herman (72-21-19)   WDEC15   New York, New York, USA
               (World Featherweight Championship)
Aug. 27, 1925   Babe Herman (72-20-19)   D15   **Waterbury, Co**nnecticut, USA
               (World Featherweight Championship)

Jan. 2, 1925   Danny Kramer (100-16-20) WTKO9   New York, New York, USA
(World Featherweight Championship)

Lou Brouillard

Nov. 30, 1933   Vince Dundee (105-14-14)   LDEC15   **Boston, Massachusetts**, USA
(NBA World & NYSAC World Middleweight Championships)
Aug. 9, 1933   Ben Jeby (48-8-4)   WKO7   New York, New York, USA
(NYSAC World Middleweight Championship)
Oct. 23, 1931   Young Jack Thompson WDEC15   **Boston, Massachusetts**, USA
(76-28-12)
(NBA World Welterweight Championship)

John Ruiz

Apr. 3, 2010   David Haye (23-1)   LTKO9   Manchester, Lancashire, UK
(WBA World Heavyweight Championship)
Aug. 30, 2010   Nikolai Valuev (48-1)   LDEC12   Prenzlauer Berg, Berlin, Germany
(vacant WBA Heavyweight Championship)
Dec. 17, 2005   Nikolai Valuev (42-0)   LDEC12   Prenzlauer Berg, Berlin, Germany
(WBA Heavyweight Championship)
Nov. 13, 2004   Andrew Golota (38-4-1)   WDEC12   New York, New York, USA
(WBA Heavyweight Championship)
Apr. 17, 2004   Hasim Rahman (35-4-1)   WDEC12   Atlantic City, New Jersey, USA
(WBA Interim Heavyweight Championship)
Mar. 1, 2003   Roy Jones, Jr. (47-1)   LDEC12   Las Vegas, Nevada, USA
(WBA Heavyweight Championship)
July 27, 2002   Kirk Johnson (32-0-1)   WDQ10   Las Vegas, Nevada, USA
(WBA Heavyweight Championship)
Dec. 15, 2001   Evander Holyfield (37-5-1)   D12   **Mashantucket, Connecticut**, USA
(WBA Heavyweight Championship)
Mar. 3, 2001   Evander Holyfield (37-4-1)   WDEC12   Las Vegas, Nevada, USA
(WBA Heavyweight Championship)
Aug. 12, 2000   Evander Holyfield (36-4-1)   LDEC12   Las Vegas, Nevada, USA
(vacant WBA Heavyweight Championship)

George Dixon

Nov. 9, 1903 Pedlar Palmer (37-5-1)   WDEC20 Newcastle, Tune and Wear, UK
              (World Featherweight Championship)
Jan. 9, 1900 Terry McGovern (41-2-3)   LTKO8   New York, New York, USA
              (World Featherweight Championship)
Nov. 21, 1899 Eddie Lenny (15-6-23)   WDEC25 Brooklyn, New York, USA
              (World Featherweight Championship)
Nov. 2, 1899 Will Curley (5-1)   WDEC25 Brooklyn, New York, USA
              (World Featherweight Championship)
Aug. 11, 1999 Eddie Santry (21-3-4)   WDEC6   Chicago, Illinois, USA
              (World Featherweight Championship)
July 11, 1899 Tommy White (35-7-26)   WDEC20 Denver, Colorado, USA
              (World Featherweight Championship)
July 3, 1899 Sam Bolen (20-7-16)   WKO3   Louisville, Kentucky, USA
              (World Featherweight Championship)
June 2, 1899 Joe Bernstein (13-7-16)   WDEC25 Brooklyn, New York, USA
              (World Featherweight Championship)
May 15, 1899 Kid Broad (8-3-7)   WDEC20 Buffalo, New York, USA
              (World Featherweight Championship)
Jan. 17, 1899 Young Pluto (16-5-16)   WKO10   New York, New York, USA
              (World Featherweight Championship)
Nov. 29, 1998 Oscar Gardner (62-5-19)   WDEC25 New York, New York, USA
              (World Featherweight Championship)
Nov. 11, 1898 Dave Sullivan (17-1-7)   WDQ10   New York, New York, USA
              (World Featherweight Championship)
Oct. 4, 1897 Solly Smith (27-4-12)   LDEC20 San Francisco, California, USA
              (World Featherweight Championship)
Mar. 24, 1897 Frank Erne (18-1-11)   WDEC25 Brooklyn, New York, USA
              (World Featherweight Championship)
Jan. 22, 1897 Torpedo Billy Murphy   WKO6   Brooklyn, New York, USA
              (97-30-22)
              (World Featherweight Championship)
Nov. 27, 1896 Frank Erne (17-0-11)   LDEC20 New York, New York, USA
              (World Featherweight Championship)
Sept. 25, 1896 Tommy White (17-4-12)   D20   New York, New York, USA
              (World Featherweight Championship)

Sept. 25, 1893   Solly Smith (16-2-3)   WTKO7   Brooklyn, New York, USA
                 (World Featherweight Championship)
Aug. 7, 1893   Eddie Pierce (1-0-1)   WTKO3   Brooklyn, New York, USA
                 (World Featherweight Championship)
July 28, 1891   Abe Willis (8-1-12)   WKO5   San Francisco, California, USA
                 (World Bantamweight Championship)
Mar. 31, 1891   Cal McCarthy (10-0-3)   WTKO22   Troy, New York, USA
                 (World Featherweight Championship)
Oct. 23, 1890   Johnny Murphy (2-2-2)   WKO40   Providence, Rhode Island, USA
                 (World Featherweight Championship)
June 27, 1890   Nunc Wallace (6-2)   WRTD19   Soho, London, UK
                 (World Featherweight Championship)

Joe Walcott

Nov. 29, 1906   Honey Mellody (33-7-10)   LTKO2   **Chelsea, Massachusetts**, USA
                 (World Welterweight Championship)
Oct. 16, 1906   Honey Mellody (32-7-10)   LDEC15   **Chelsea, Massachusetts**, USA
                 (World Welterweight Championship)
Sept. 29, 1906   Billy Rhodes (7-2-1)   D20   Kansas City, Missouri, USA
                 (World Welterweight Championship)
July 10, 1906   Jack Dougherty (28-8-8)   WKO2   **Chelsea, Massachusetts**, USA
                 (World Welterweight Championship)
Sept. 5, 1904   Sam Langford (21-2-10)   D15   **Manchester, New Hampshire**, USA
                 (World Welterweight Championship)
Apr. 29, 1904   Dixie Kid (21-8-6)   LDQ20   San Francisco, California, USA
                 (World Welterweight Championship)
July 3, 1903   Mose LaFontise (24-6-5)   WKO3   Butte, Montana, USA
                 (World Welterweight Championship)
June 18, 1903   Young Peter Jackson (58-17-18) D20 Portland, Oregon, USA
                 (World Welterweight Championship)
June 23, 1902   Tommy West (30-11-9)   WDEC15   Covent Gardens, London, UK
                 (World Welterweight Championship)
Dec. 18, 1901   Rube Ferns (34-2-5)   WDEC15   Fort Erie, Ontario, Canada

(World Welterweight Championship)

Oct. 29, 1897 George Lavigne (32-2-10) LTKO12 San Francisco, California, USA

Demetrius Andrade

Nov. 19, 2021 Jason Quigley (19-1) WTKO2 **Manchester, New Hampshire**, USA
(WBO World Middleweight Championship)

Apr. 17, 2021 Liam Williams (23-2-1) WDEC12 Hollywood, Florida, USA
(WBO World Middleweight Championship)

Jan. 30, 2020 Luke Keller (17-2-1) WTKO9 Miami, Illinois, USA
(WBO World Middleweight Championship)

June 29, 2019 Maciej Sulecki (28-1) WDEC12 **Providence, Rhode Island**, USA
(WBO World Middleweight Championship)

Jan. 18, 2019 Artur Akavov (19-2) WTKO2 New York, New York, USA,
(WBO World Middleweight Championship)

Oct. 20, 2018 Walter Kautondokwa (17-0) WDEC12 **Boston, Massachusetts**, USA
(WBO World Middleweight Championship)

Mar. 11, 2017 Jack Culcay (22-1) WDEC12 Ludwigshafen, Germany
(WBA World Super Welterweight Championship)

June 14, 2014 Brian Rose (25-1-1) WTKO7 Brooklyn, New York, USA
(WBA World Super Welterweight Championship)

Nov. 9, 2013 Vanes Martirosyan (33-0-1) WDEC12 Corpus Christi, Texas, USA
(WBA World Super Welterweight Championship)

Jack Delaney

Dec. 10, 1926 Jamaica Kid (20-50-10) WTKO3 **Waterbury, Connecticut**, USA
(NYSAC World Lightweight Championship)

July 16, 1926 Paul Berlenbach (31-2-3) WDEC15 Brooklyn, New York, USA
(NYSAC World Light Heavyweight Championship)

Dec. 11, 1925 Paul Berlenbach (28-1-2) WDEC15 New York, New York, USA

Battling Battalino

Nov. 4, 1931 Earl Mastro (49-3-2) WDEC10 Chicago, Illinois, USA
(NBA World Featherweight Championship)

July 23, 1931 Freddie Miller (86-4-3) WDEC10 Cincinnati, Ohio, USA
(NBA World Featherweight Championship)

May 22, 1931 Fidel LaBarba (48-8-7) WDEC15 New York, New York, USA
(NYSAC World Featherweight Championship)

Dec. 12, 1930 Kid Chocolate (57-2-1) WDEC15 New York, New York, USA
(NYSAC World Featherweight Championship)

July 15, 1930 Ignacio Fernandez (32-21-10) WKO5 **East Hartford, Connecticut**, USA
(World Featherweight Championship)

Sept. 23, 1929 Andre Routis (56-23-7) WDEC15 **East Hartford, Connecticut**, USA

Travis Simms

Nov. 7, 2007 Joachim Alcine (28-0) LDEC12 **Bridgeport, Connecticut**, USA
(WBA World Super Welterweight Championship)

Jan. 6, 2007 Jose Antonio Rivera (38-4-1) WTKO9 Hollywood, Florida, USA
(WBA World Super Welterweight Championship)

Oct. 2, 2004 Bronco McKart (47-5) WDEC12 New York, New York, USA
(WBA World Super Welterweight Championship)

Dec. 13, 2003 Alejandro Garcia (22-0), WKO5 Atlantic City, New Jersey, USA
(WBA World Super Welterweight Championship)

Joey Gamache

Dec. 10, 1994 Orzubek Nazarov (19-0) LTKO11 **Portland, Maine**, USA
(WBA World Lightweight Championship)

Oct. 24, 1992 Tony Lopez (40-3-1) LTKO11 **Portland, Maine**, USA
(WBA World Lightweight Championship)

June 13, 1991 Chil Sung Jun (18-1) WTKO9 **Portland, Maine**, USA
(vacant WBA World Lightweight Championship)

June 28, 1991 Jerry Ngobeni (19-1) WTKO10 **Lewiston, Maine**, USA
(vacant WBA World Super Featherweight Championship)

Jose Antonio Rivera

Jan. 6, 2007	Travis Simms (24-0)	LTKO9	Hollywood, Florida, USA
	(WBA World Super Welterweight Championship)		
May 6, 2006	Alejandro Garcia (25-1)	WDEC12	**Worcester, MA**, USA
	(WBA World Super Welterweight Championship)		
April 2, 2005	Luis Collazo (24-1)	LDEC12	**Worcester, MA**, USA
	(WBA World Welterweight Championship)		
Sept. 13, 2003	Michel Trabant (38-0)	WDEC12	Neukölln, Germany
	(vacant WBA World Welterweight Championship)		

Micky Ward

July 9, 1997	Vince Phillips (36-3)	LTKO3	**Boston, Massachusetts**, USA
	(IBF World Super Lightweight Championship)		

THE RING'S TOP 100

7. Willie Pep

23. Marvin Hagler

38. Louis Kaplan

54. Rocky Marciano

64. Jack Sharkey

99. Louis Brouillard

Some of the boxing's all-time greatest matches involved some of New England's greatest boxers (see chart below):

> ### *THE RING* FIGHTS OF THE YEAR
>
> 1942   **Willie Pep** WDEC15 Chalky Wright I at Madison Square Garden, New York, NY (NYSAC World Featherweight Championship)
>
> 1949   **Willie Pep** WDEC15 Sandy Saddler at Madison Square Garden, New York, NY (World Featherweight Championship)

1952   **Rocky Marciano** WKO13 Jersey Joe Walcott I at Municipal Stadium, Philadelphia, PA (NBA World Heavyweight Championship)

1953   **Rocky Marciano** WKO11 Roland LaStarza at Polo Grounds, New York, NY (NBA World Heavyweight Championship)

1954   **Rocky Marciano** WKO8 Ezzard Charles II at Yankee Stadium, New York, NY (NBA World Heavyweight Championship)

1955   Carmen Basilio WKO12 **Tony DeMarco** II at **Boston Garden, Boston, MA** (World Welterweight Championship)

1985   **Marvin Hagler** WKO3 Thomas Hearns at Caesars Palace, Las Vegas, NV (WBC, WBA & IBF World Middleweight Championship)

1987   Sugar Ray Leonard W12 **Marvin Hagler** at Caesars Palace, Las Vegas, NV (WBC World Middleweight Championship)

2001   **Micky Ward** WDEC10 Emanuel Augustus at Hampton Casino, Hampton, NH

2002   **Micky Ward** WDEC10 Arturo Gatti I at **Mohegan Sun, Uncasville, CT**

2003   Arturo Gatti WDEC10 **Micky Ward** III at Boardwalk Hall, Atlantic City, NJ

2011   Victor Ortiz WDEC12 Andre Berto at **Foxwoods, Mashantucket, CT** (WBC World Welterweight Championship)

THE RING FIGHTERS OF THE YEAR

1932   Jack Sharkey

1945   Willie Pep

1952   Rocky Marciano

1954   Rocky Marciano

1955   Rocky Marciano

1983   Marvin Hagler

1985   **Marvin Hagler** (co-winner with Donald Curry)

NEW ENGLAND'S GREATEST BOXERS IN THE INTERNATIONAL BOXING HAL OF FAME

PARTICIPANTS

Modern Boxers
(last bout no later than 1989, those enshrined
1990–2014, last bout no earlier than 1943)

Marvelous Marvin Hagler
Cocoa Kid
Rocky Marciano
Willie Pep
Sandy Saddler

Old-Time Boxers
(last bout no earlier than 1893, no later than 1988)

Battling Battalino
Lou Brouillard
Jack Delaney
Tony DeMarco
George Dixon
Lous (Kid) Kaplan
Sam Langford
Jack Sharkey
(Barbados) Joe Walcott

Pioneer
(last bout prior to 1892)

John L. Sullivan

NON-PARTICIPANTS
(contributors to sport apart from boxer or observers in their particular fields)

Promoter Sam Silverman (Chelsea, MA)
Promoter Rip Valenti (Boston, MA)
Promoter/Manager Lou Viscusi (Hartford, CT)
Manager Al Weill (New London, CT)
Manager Tom O'Rourke
Trainer Freddie Roach (Dedham, MA)
Trainer Bill Gore (Providence, RI

OBSERVERS
(print and media journalists, publisher, writers, and historians)
Historian/television producer Bob Yalen (Hartford, CT)
Broadcaster Col. Bob Sheridan (Boston, MA)
Journalist Ron Borges (Oak Bluffs, MA)
Journalist George Kimball (Boston, MA)
Journalist Dan Parker (Waterbury, CT)
A. J. Liebling (Providence, RI)

PHOTO GALLERY LAYOUT & CREDITS

Willie Pep

(L-R) – Muhammad Ali & Marvin Hagler

(L) Sandy Saddler & Larry Boardman

John L. Sullivan

Vinny Pazienza

Tony DeMarco

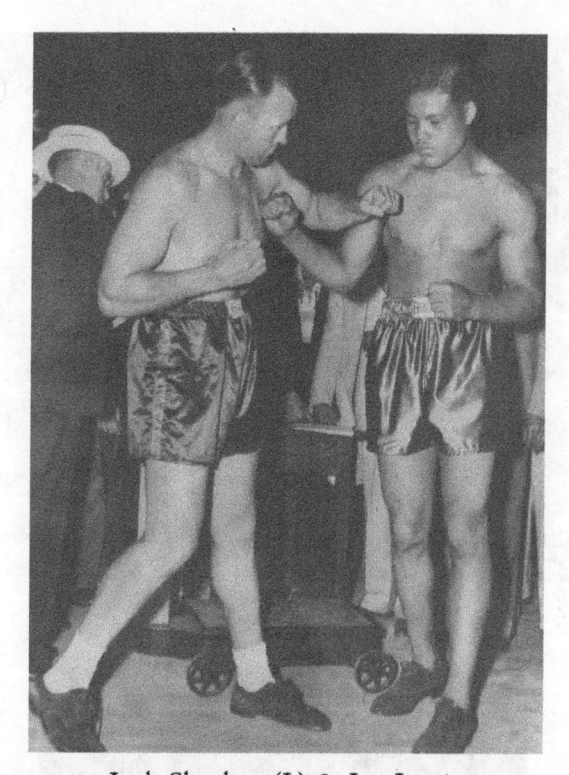

Jack Sharkey (L) & Joe Louis

Paul Pender (L) & Terry Downes

Chad Dawson (L)

John Ruiz

Demetrius Andrade (L)

Travis Simms

Jose Antonio Rivera

Micky Ward

Photo Credits:

COVER SHOT: Hogan Bassey & Willie Pep (R) – photo courtesy of Fightography

Emily Harney: Vinny Pazienza, Tony DeMarco, Chad Dawson, John Ruiz, Demetrius Andrade, Travis Simms, Jose Antonio Rivera, Micky Ward

Fightography: Willie Pep (2 including cover shot), Sandy Saddler, Paul Pender, Jack Sharkey

Angie Carlino: Marvin Hagler

Getty Images: John L. Sullivan